T0274377

SEARCHING FOR MAYFLOWERS

The Story of Canada's First Quintuplets

LORI MCKAY

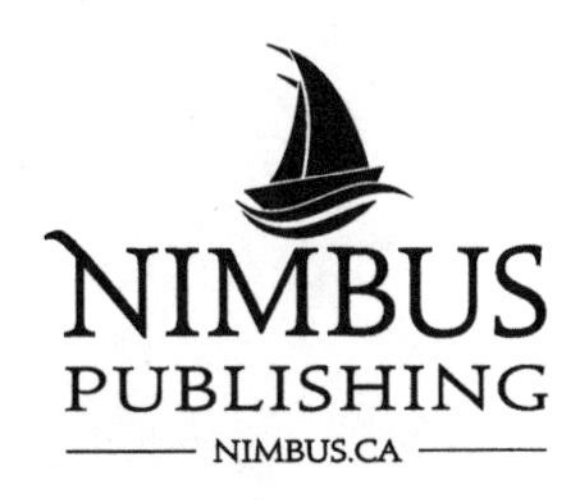

Nimbus Publishing Limited
3660 Strawberry Hill Street, Halifax, NS, B3K 5A9
(902) 455-4286 nimbus.ca

Printed and bound in Canada

NB1736

Editor: Stephanie Domet
Editor for the press: Angela Mombourquette
Cover design: Heather Bryan
Interior design: Jenn Embree

Nimbus Publishing is based in Kjipuktuk, Mi'kma'ki, the traditional territory of the Mi'kmaq People.

Library and Archives Canada Cataloguing in Publication

Title: Searching for mayflowers : the true story of Canada's first quintuplets / Lori McKay.
Names: McKay, Lori, author.
Identifiers: Canadiana (print) 20240386973 | Canadiana (ebook) 20240387015 | ISBN 9781774713303 (softcover) | ISBN 9781774713310 (EPUB)
Subjects: LCSH: Quintuplets—Nova Scotia—Biography. | LCGFT: Biographies.
Classification: LCC CT9998.M8 M35 2024 | DDC 971.6/03092555—dc23

Nimbus Publishing acknowledges the financial support for its publishing activities from the Government of Canada, the Canada Council for the Arts, and from the Province of Nova Scotia. We are pleased to work in partnership with the Province of Nova Scotia to develop and promote our creative industries for the benefit of all Nova Scotians.

CONTENTS

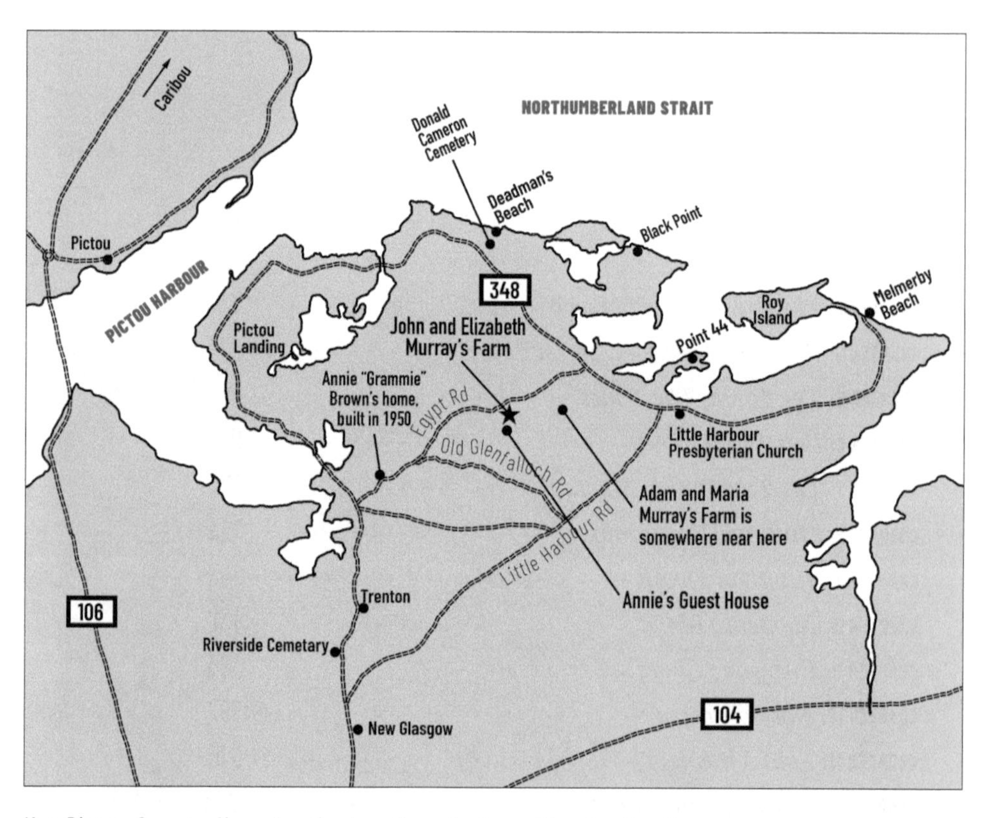

Key Pictou County, Nova Scotia, locations in ***Searching for Mayflowers***.

CHAPTER 1: THE STORY

My grandmother Annie lived in the smallest house I've ever been in. It was a tiny home before tiny homes were a thing. The house had a cramped little kitchen with a table for two, one small bedroom, and a closet-sized bathroom with a thick plastic screen for a door. All the walls were panelled in wood and the entire place smelled of bleach—she washed everything in it, from her dishes to her floors to her clothes.

My brother and I liked going to her place for visits because she always fed us dessert for meals. Our mother would drop us off and then run errands. She'd pick us up a few hours later and take us home with bellyaches.

The day my grandmother first told us the story of the Murray quintuplets was no exception. We sat in her sparsely decorated living room eating gingerbread smothered in her secret-recipe lemon sauce and watching inappropriate afternoon soap operas on her miniature black-and-white television.

"Pass me that brown album," she said to me, pointing to the stand where she kept her stack of *National Enquirer* newspapers, her Bible, and her picture albums. "I want to show you something."

I pulled out the heavy, well-worn album and handed it to her. Then, before I knew what was happening, she yanked me up onto her lap. She liked when we sat on her knee, but I didn't. I was seven and too old for knee-sitting. I quickly squirmed over to the sheet-covered armrest of her giant comfy swivel chair. She began flipping through the pages, past school pictures of me and my brother and our many cousins. She paused for a moment on a black-and-white picture of a young woman on a horse.

"Wasn't I beautiful?" she asked, tapping the picture with her slightly crooked index finger.

I nodded, although it was hard to make the connection between the young, lithe, fair-haired girl with the lovely smile, and the old lady beside me. She was still an attractive woman, but she was certainly no longer thin, and her current rosy complexion was obviously painted on. Round pink circles decorated her high cheekbones like dainty apples.

Annie Margaret (Murray) Brown in her youth.

Grammie continued flipping pages and didn't stop again until near the back.

"Here it is," she said.

Under a thin layer of plastic film was an old, yellowed newspaper clipping. The headline on the article—dated 1937 in blue pen at the top—read: "Nova Scotia's Only Quintuplets." Accompanying the story was a picture of five babies lined up in a row.

"When this photo was taken," she said, "four of the babies were dead but the one on the left was still alive."

It was morbid, and fascinating. I leaned in to scrutinize and memorize the details. The photo was old, but the babies' features were still clearly visible. They wore white christening dresses, their little hands poking out of the sleeves, some with fingers balled up into tiny fists. The baby on the left was different. His or her eyes were gentler, and you could see creases at the corners. There was

John R. P. Fraser's photo of the Murray quintuplets. In this image, only the baby at the far left is still living. Note that a hand is in the frame holding the sleeping baby next to its siblings.

also a grown-up's hand and arm in the picture, which seemed to be holding the living child up beside the others. The adult-size fingers also offered some perspective to their diminutive size.

This living baby's name was Jeanette Rankin Murray. She was the first-born quintuplet, the smallest, and she lived the longest—just three days.

Grammie paused a moment to warn my brother, who was six, not to spill lemon sauce or drop crumbs on her sofa. "As soon as you eat it all, I'll cut you another slice," she added.

She worried almost fanatically that we weren't getting enough to eat. She used to call our house daily to make sure we weren't hungry. Her concern had no basis. My brother and I were perfectly healthy, well-cared-for children, and the daily calls and food obsession drove my mother crazy, especially since if my grandmother had her way we would be as plump and round as she was. As kids, whenever Mom would deny us a treat, we'd threaten to call Grammie. If we followed through on that threat, she would arrive at our house within the hour with a case of store-bought jarred applesauce—her usual treat of choice—or occasionally a case of chocolate bars.

"The babies were born right here in Little Egypt in 1880," Grammie continued, pausing a moment to do some mental math. "That was 102 years ago."

When you're seven, a hundred years is an almost unimaginable amount of time. A hundred years was before my grandmother was even born. The story she was telling me felt like a story from a make-believe place, a fairy tale.

"The farm was just a five-minute drive up the road," she continued. "The family is a distant relative, and it was your great-great-grandmother Elizabeth Murray who delivered them."

She went on to explain that after the babies died, just days after their birth, famous circus showman P. T. Barnum tried to purchase the bodies so he could mummify them for his show. Fearing grave robbers, the Murrays moved the babies' bodies from the local cemetery to the cellar of their home for three months before burying them elsewhere.

"It became a family secret," she said. "Today, no one knows for sure where they were finally laid to rest."

It was the most fascinating real-life story I had ever heard, and we had a family connection to it. I was proud and immensely curious. Every time my grandmother and I were together in the months after that, I peppered her with questions about those babies. Where *might* they be buried? Could she guess? Why was the grave location a secret? And why would the circus want to buy dead babies? My grandmother told me what she knew, which was very little. Just tidbits of information passed down to her by her grandmother and great-aunts.

"It was the women in the family who spoke of such things as births and babies," she told me. "The women were the keepers of all the family stories."

"I'm going to write a book about the quintuplets someday," I told my grandmother during one of our chats.

"That's a wonderful idea," she said. She probably didn't take me seriously; it was merely a whimsical declaration from a kid, after all. Still, I never forgot saying those words and a plan began to take shape in the back of my mind.

When I would tell people about the Murray quintuplets—which I did often as a child, and even as an adult—the response I would typically get was, "Wow. I had no idea!" People were always interested though. They knew of the famous Dionne quintuplets from

Callander, Ontario—who were worldwide media sensations in the 1930s and '40s—but not the Murray quints of Nova Scotia, who were born a half-century before.

Because I was telling them something they'd never heard elsewhere, I began to feel a kind of ownership of the story. No one was talking about them except me. I can't say for sure that this one remarkable tale fuelled my entire educational and professional future, but I know it played a significant part. It was the first instance I remember of ever wanting to retell something to the masses. It motivated me to become a writer. I studied journalism in university and then worked in the newspaper and magazine industries for decades. The story of the quintuplets lingered in the back of my mind the entire time. So why did it take me so long to write this book? For one thing, I didn't know how. How does one write about something with so little information? And how did I write about something I had held on such a pedestal for most of my life?

It wasn't until I was in my forties that I realized my window to write a book was closing. My grandmother was gone, my mother was nearing seventy, and her sisters were in their eighties. They wouldn't be around forever to answer my questions and to share their memories. It had to be now, or it would probably be never.

The first thing I needed to do was figure out what story I wanted to tell.

Many years after my grandmother showed me that old newspaper clipping, when I was in my late teens, I remember sitting cross-legged on her living room floor and reading through her news clippings about the wondrous babies for myself.

One article, published in the New Glasgow *Evening News* in the 1960s, was based on files from the *Eastern Chronicle*, the local weekly newspaper in 1880. It began:

> *It was a cold blustery Sunday morning, Feb. 15, 1880, the temperature near zero, when a messenger called at the home of Dr.*

Wm. Fraser of New Glasgow. The doctor was wanted at the home of Adam Murray, who resided in Egypt, a tiny settlement four miles away. They already had seven children and Mrs. Murray was again confined. Could the Dr. come right away? Comments on the weather were exchanged as the Dr.'s horse was hitched and he prepared to attend a case of childbirth at the Murray home. To the tune of jingling sleigh bells the Dr. was off. After a brisk ride over the snow-covered lonely roads, Dr. Fraser arrived at the Murrays'. There was the usual note of excitement in the home as the Dr. arrived. Within an hour, Mrs. Murray presented her husband with five children.

I remember thinking, "Hey, wait just a minute. This isn't how the story goes." There was no mention whatsoever of my great-great-grandmother who delivered the quintuplets.

"Why isn't your Grandma Murray mentioned?" I asked Grammie.

"I don't know," she said, pondering my question as if it were the first time she'd ever considered it. "All I know is that Grandma told us the doctor came later, after they were born. I think maybe it's just how it was at that time. Women didn't always get the credit they deserved."

This realization took root in my mind. Over the years, as I sought information on the story of the Murray quintuplets, I always looked for some mention of my great-great-grandmother's role in it. I read books such as James M. Cameron's *Wreck of the Melmerby and Other Pictou County Stories* and Clyde F. Macdonald's *Notable Events in Pictou County*, as well as other "on this date in time" articles in local newspapers, but the story was always the same: the doctor delivered the babies. No mention of Elizabeth Murray. People always recalled the events of the birth based on that one initial story that was published in the *Eastern Chronicle* days after the quintuplets were born.

I imagine the Murrays—simple country folks who were far from media savvy even by the standards of their day. They would not have bothered or even thought to contact the paper with the correct information.

It frustrated me. Unless my great-great-grandmother was lying—and I doubt she was, as she was always described to me as a much-loved and respected family matriarch—the official story that was on the record, the one that people outside our family knew, was, at best, incomplete, and in all likelihood, wrong.

I grew up in a family of women. My mother has five half-sisters and no brothers. Most of those women have daughters. Looking at five generations—starting with my great-grandparents and ending with my own generation—my family tree includes almost twice the number of females as males. When I picture the relatives on my mother's side, the Murray side, I think of a group of blond-haired, blue-eyed women and girls. (I am one of the few brunettes in the mix.)

Relationships between the women in a family are always important. But a "sisterhood" was especially crucial back in 1880—in fact, it was a matter of survival. When the quintuplets were born, there was no hospital in Pictou County. Although there were doctors, most women in rural areas—especially poor farming families like the Murrays—would call on a neighbour, relative, or local midwife to help with a home delivery.

Learning how to deliver a baby was a necessity for women. They were taught by their mothers, sisters, aunts, neighbours, and local practising midwives. My great-great-grandmother Elizabeth

Murray (my grandmother's grandmother) was not trained in any official capacity, but she was a wife and mother herself and had helped deliver many babies in the community over the years. It just made sense to me that Maria, the mother of the quintuplets, would call on her closest neighbour—Elizabeth—when her labour pains began.

So why was she left out of the story?

There were many times throughout my research when I found myself desperately wishing I could step back in time to the day in question: February 15, 1880. If only I could accurately record all the details of the birth, the family, and the era. But as much as I wish this were possible, I would never want to stay in the past for any real span of time. Not because I'd miss medical advances, the internet, and other modern conveniences—although I would surely feel the loss of such things—but because I would not be able to tolerate a nineteenth-century woman's place in society. Women's accomplishments and contributions have long been cast aside and forgotten in so many aspects of human history. Consider Emily Stowe (1831–1903), the first female doctor to practise in Canada, or Cairine Wilson (1885–1962), Canada's first female senator. Too few people are familiar with these names, let alone their achievements.

I'm not saying my great-great-grandmother was any kind of hero; I'm just saying she was there and her existence in this story is missing.

All that remains in the archives are the names of men who played a role in this story: the doctor, Dr. William Fraser; the pharmacist, James Jackson; and the photographer, John R. P. Fraser. The *Eastern Chronicle*'s article even phrased the miracle as, "Within an hour, Mrs. Murray presented her husband with five children." As if the children were a wonderful surprise she produced out of nowhere and then gifted to him. There's no mention of the nine long months she likely endured, filled with discomfort and the inherent risks to her health and even her life, nor of the challenging and painful labour.

As the bones of this book started to come together, I realized I was in pursuit of several things. Yes, I wanted to unravel the mysteries surrounding the babies and recognize the women in the tale, but there was also something more. Woven into my journey was a deeper purpose: preservation. I needed to keep the story alive, as well as the people in it. My kids didn't know my grandmother, so when my generation—my brother, cousins, and I—are gone, so is she. And so are her fascinating stories. At some point in the future, the same fate awaits me. The thought of all these memories fading into obscurity unsettles me. I wanted a record for posterity.

And when it came to my retelling of the Murray quintuplet story, I wanted to tell not only the story of the miraculous birth, but of my family connection to it.

But how did I tell this story, beyond what was captured in the official record? No one alive today knows what really occurred back in 1880 in Little Egypt, Nova Scotia. There are no journals or family papers that capture the details and facts. And many of the documents that do exist contain inconsistencies and inaccurate information. But there are family memories and stories, and so, where recorded facts don't offer details, I have crafted scenes and fleshed out historical narratives, drawing on research to arrive at a dramatic approximation of what might have happened. I applied the same approach to recreate scenes involving my grandmother, Annie, in the 1930s, '40s, '50s and '60s. Wherever possible, I note the facts that are part of the historical record, while recognizing its limitations in fully capturing the reality of the lives of the women who came before me.

LITTLE EGYPT, 1880: THE BIRTH

In the early morning hours of February 15, 1880, thirty-three-year-old Maria Murray went into labour. It had been a difficult pregnancy for the busy farmwife and mother of five. She was larger and more uncomfortable than with her previous pregnancies, and her responsibilities with the children and the farm had been hard those last few weeks. She was anxious for the baby to be born.

The family's little farmhouse was always crowded but felt especially so in winter when the cold and blustery weather forced everyone indoors. Their household consisted of Maria and her husband, Adam, and the couple's five children, along with Adam's two older sons from his first marriage. As Adam was an only child, it's possible his elderly father, Thomas, eighty-two, lived with the family as well.

On that particular morning, Elizabeth Murray—Maria's neighbour, friend, and relative by marriage—was there to help deliver the expected new baby. Elizabeth's eldest son, Tom, eleven, may have been there too. It had been the middle of the night when the knock came to Elizabeth's door to help, and Tom had agreed to escort his mother across the fields between the two properties. (One of my aunts recalled that Great-Uncle Tom claimed he was the only one of his siblings to see the babies. Since they were not the type of family to visit with the neighbours, at best guess, Tom was there with his mother when they were born.)

As Maria's labour intensified, her family did their best to help in small ways. Someone kept the big wood stove full in the centre of the little farmhouse kitchen, and a pot of water boiling. There was always an extra stack of dry wood nearby. They gathered what clean, unused blankets they had, which didn't amount to many. The house was warm if you were near the stove, but the windows were drafty and the walls poorly insulated. Elizabeth sat by the labouring woman's side in the parlour off the kitchen—which had been transformed to a birth room—and offered words of encouragement.

Outside, the temperature was well below freezing, about -17ºC by some records. With the area's proximity to the ocean, the onshore wind in the open field was biting. It was the damp kind of cold that gets into your bones. The ground was covered with a deep, heavy snow. This was typical winter weather for Nova Scotia.

Although Elizabeth had helped deliver several healthy children over the years, she understood the dangers of childbirth and knew there were countless things that could go wrong. If the infant became stuck in the birth canal or distressed, for example, there was little she could do to save either the child or the mother. She had no anesthesia or pain medications to offer Maria during her labour.

Maria was a tall, healthy woman who carried her pregnancy well. Although she was larger than normal this time around, she was only expecting one baby. No one knew it at the time, but she had many factors in her favour that could lead to a multiple birth. Multiples are more likely when there are other multiples in the family, and Maria's mother had given birth to three sets of twins among her eighteen children. Multiples are also more likely to be born to a woman who is over thirty years of age (Maria was thirty-three according to one census report, although another census lists her as twenty-eight at the time of the birth), is tall with a high body mass index (which fit her description), and has already had numerous births (Maria had given birth eight times before).

It was sometimes customary to educate the younger generations, so Elizabeth invited Maria's eldest daughter, ten-year-old Christina—Tena for short—to be at her mother's side, where she could offer support and learn at the same time.

Elizabeth would have frequently checked Maria's progress during labour. As the birth drew nearer, she likely desired another set of hands to assist. She asked one of the men or boys to fetch Flora Chisholm, another neighbour known for her midwifery skills. (I learned of Flora's possible presence at the birth from someone who heard about it from other community members—another family story passed down in yet another family.) Elizabeth was as prepared as anyone could be, yet there was no way for her to anticipate what was to come.

Together, Flora and Elizabeth helped Maria give birth to a tiny baby girl.

It was not likely known exactly how many weeks Maria was along in her pregnancy, but they had no reason to expect anything other than a healthy, average-size baby, especially given that Maria had put on a hefty amount of baby weight. So the size of the infant was a shock, and the midwives were immediately concerned.

Elizabeth checked her quickly and wrapped the quiet infant in a blanket. Premature babies are typically quieter and less active than strong healthy babies, and this was the case with the Murray baby. Tena took the swaddled infant closer to the warmth of the fire to keep her warm.

Surprisingly, Maria was still experiencing contractions. Before anyone knew what was happening, she gave birth to a second baby. Twins, the women thought. This child was also very small.

Elizabeth asked one of the children to inform Adam, who was outside in the barn. In those days, when babies were coming into this world, men would typically make themselves scarce. She also asked to have someone hook up a sleigh and go in town. Twins were reason enough to call the doctor. One of Adam's older sons, or perhaps a neighbour, then travelled across the snow-covered fields and back roads into the town of New Glasgow to get word to the doctor.

Meanwhile, in the little Murray home, Maria was still experiencing labour pains, and within minutes a third baby was born.

And then a fourth.

There were no more blankets, so someone took the green cloth blinds with the little gold tassels down from the windows. They would have to do. The blinds became the fourth baby's swaddle. Outside those windows, the wind and snow howled around the tiny farmhouse in Little Egypt.

Then a fifth baby was born.

CHAPTER 2:

THE MURRAYS

A few summers ago, my husband and I were invited to visit a neighbour's cottage to see their pet bird, which had travelled with them on vacation from Ontario. The cottage was shared by several siblings in their family who took turns staying there in the summers. I'd always been curious to see inside. The place is well over a century old and had been there long before all the other cottages that populated that area of northern Nova Scotia's coast.

The bird, as it turned out, had full reign of the cottage, and flew wherever it wanted, periodically landing on humans. It was cute and mildly entertaining, but I was far more interested in the cottage itself, which was filled with cozy furniture, antiques, and memorabilia from the area. I paused when I came to a particularly interesting frame on the wall. Under yellowed glass was the title "Hector Passengers," followed by a list of names. The ship *Hector* was a merchant vessel known for its historic significance as it made the first recorded arrival of Scottish immigrants to Nova Scotia in 1773.

I recognized all the family names on the list. (As it happens, the name of the family whose cottage I stood in was not among them, but clearly there was a connection. It's a two-degrees-of-*Hector* kind of thing in Pictou County.)

There were ten Murrays listed, as well as several McKays and Pattersons (my paternal grandparents), plus the last names of many of my cousins, friends, and neighbours: Cameron, Chisholm, Fraser, Grant, McDonald, McLean, etc. Looking at that list proudly framed on the wall was the first time I truly recognized the connection between present-day Pictou County and its original families. It's a link that continues today, two and a half centuries later, even though most younger generations have no idea it exists.

The ship *Hector* landed on the shores of Pictou Harbour, Nova Scotia, on September 15, 1773. Often compared to the celebrated American ship the *Mayflower*, the *Hector* voyage was significant not only because it was the first to bring a substantial number of Scottish Highlanders to the country, but also because its passengers experienced great tragedy at sea. Theirs was a tale of survival against the odds.

The Scottish people immigrated to Nova Scotia out of necessity. They were, essentially, homeless in their own country after the Highlanders were defeated by the British at the Battle of Culloden in 1746. The clan system the Scots lived by—extended family and kinship under the same surname—was nearly destroyed by the colonizing British. The tartans and kilts that had always been a source of family pride were forbidden. Many clan chiefs were killed, and their houses burned to the ground or sold to English farmers. New laws made it illegal for a Highlander to even play the bagpipes, as they were considered a weapon that inspired troops and intimidated enemies. During this period, many Scots were forced to flee the country, and that time in history is referred to as the Highland Clearances. The exodus continued until the mid-nineteenth century.

Advertisements in Scotland for the *Hector* passage promised a new life in a new world. Adults were offered passage on the *Hector* at a cost of three pounds five shillings—a veritable bargain at the time—kids travelled at a discounted rate, and babies travelled for free. The emigrants were promised free provisions for a year and coastal farmland. This all sounded good—probably too good—but it was still a difficult decision for them to make. Once they left, they would not likely ever return to their homeland.

Those who accepted the offer were mostly poor crop farmers and artisans who spoke only Gaelic. Many of the travellers were from Loch Broom and nearby Sutherland. (Today, there are communities in Pictou County named Loch Broom and Sutherland's River, among many other Scottish names.)

No official record of passengers was made at the time of sailing, but on a list compiled years later from travellers' memories, the *Hector* carried 189 Scots—made up of 33 families, 25 single men, and one bagpiper (who apparently travelled for free because the others wanted him there for entertainment and to raise spirits)—plus ten crew and the captain, for a total of 200.

More than twenty years old, the *Hector* was a three-masted cargo ship meant for freight and short hauls, not transporting people across the vast and unpredictable Atlantic Ocean. It left Loch Broom, Scotland, on July 8, 1773, destined for a place called Pictou in North America. The area was named by the Mi'kmaq people who had lived on the land for thousands of years. They called it "Pictook," which means "exploding gas." The name was likely related to the coal fields in the area and methane that bubbled up from the seams below the harbour. (The interpretation of the name varies, and different sources provide slightly different explanations for the origin of "Pictou.")

For the first few weeks of the *Hector*'s voyage, the weather was fine, and people spent time on deck. But in August, the ship ran into a hurricane off the coast of Newfoundland that sent them off course and almost halfway back to Scotland. The passengers were forced to stay below deck, where they became plagued with seasickness, dysentery (a sometimes-fatal intestinal inflammation), and smallpox (a deadly infectious disease leading to fever and a progressive skin rash). Eighteen people died, mostly children. Their bodies were wrapped in canvas and slipped over the side. (The ships carrying these early Scottish settlers were sometimes referred to as coffin ships. As so many people would die during these long passages, it's said that sharks would follow, waiting for a body to be thrown overboard.)

A trip that was supposed to take six weeks took close to eleven. The delay forced their already thin rations of water and food—provisions such as salted beef, potatoes, barley, and oatmeal—even thinner, and they barely made it to shore alive. But those who did founded the town and county of Pictou, which affectionately became known as the Birthplace of New Scotland.

While it's difficult to imagine how bad the conditions were for those passengers, it's possible to get a rough idea of the ship itself by visiting the replica of the *Hector*, which was launched in Pictou Harbour in 2000. Built to commemorate the town's heritage, the replica took ten years to construct and involved years of fundraising and thousands of volunteer hours. The replica *Hector*'s launch on September 17, 2000, was a momentous occasion attended by more than twenty thousand cheering spectators. It has been a draw for thousands of tourists each year—often Scots who visit to understand more of their heritage. Even King Charles and Queen Consort Camilla (back when they were a prince and duchess) toured the *Hector* during their 2014 Canadian tour.

Though I remember watching the official launch ceremony on the evening news back in 2000—and had driven past the ship in the harbour many times since—I never saw it up close until the summer of 2018 when I finally took a tour. It's a common human failing to overlook things we see often; our eyes simply pass over them. And although the idea of visiting the ship had occurred to me many times—given my appreciation for local history—it wasn't something my friends or family were eager to do with me. The fact that Scottish heritage played almost a non-existent role in our upbringing no doubt fed into this lack of interest. I don't even remember learning about the *Hector* and its passengers in school, although I'm sure we must have at some point. The province's population would look quite different today without this one significant crossing. And personally speaking, almost every branch of my family tree stems back to Pictou and the ships that brought my ancestors to Nova Scotia.

Finally, I was making the effort to explore my family's past, and it turns out there's plenty to discover when you play tourist in your hometown.

My visit took place on a perfect Nova Scotia summer day—sunny and warm, with a cool breeze blowing off the water. I parked in front of an ice cream stand that was almost obscured behind a long line of loud and excited children. The smell of the sea was strong in the air and the waterfront was buzzing with tourists. The appeal to visitors was obvious; the historic seaside town of Pictou is charming with its old stone structures and brightly coloured buildings, shops, and restaurants.

Approaching the Hector Heritage Quay (pronounced "key," a quay is a place for loading and unloading boats on a waterway), I caught my first closeup view of the ship. It's an impressive landmark with its high masts and bright blue, red, and yellow paint. If it wasn't for the large pulp mill spewing foul clouds of smoke into the air directly across the harbour, the scene would have made a perfect postcard.

Other people were arriving at the same time, all clearly tourists: a bus tour of Japanese sightseers, a French-speaking couple, and a family clad in matching red tartan kilts. The foyer of the museum where I paid my $8 admission was spacious with a high ceiling. The air was scented with freshly cut wood. A recording of bagpipe music was playing in a nearby room, and I could hear the creaking of the tethered ship as it rocked on the waves outside. On the walls of the gallery hung banners of Scottish tartans representing the families who had travelled on the *Hector*; each tartan bore the clan's name below it. I easily found the tartan labelled Murray: dark green, navy blue, black, and red.

After completing the walking tour of the interpretive centre and learning much about Scottish immigration to Canada, I followed the other museum sightseers outside the back door where we found our true reason for visiting: the ship.

I first checked out the captain's quarters, which was the only sheltered area on the deck. I walked up a few steps and ducked my head to go through the tiny door (this is notable because I'm only five foot two). The compact space included a small two-bench table built into the wall and a few windows. There was no bed, but I imagined a hammock hanging in the corner. When I came out, the tourist family with the matching red kilts was coming up from below the deck. I looked down. Although I wanted to see it, I felt claustrophobic just peeking into the dark space at the bottom of the ladder. But that was what I had come to see. It was there in the belly of this ship—or rather, a ship just like it—that the first Scottish settlers endured their harrowing Atlantic crossing. And it was that crossing that helped form the foundation of the town, county, province, and in some ways, the country.

As I carefully climbed down, I could hear the water lapping loudly on the sides of the boat. It felt as though the *Hector* was cruising along the waves, even though it was securely tied to the dock. No portholes or windows meant no natural light below deck. The place smelled bad. Like damp, decay, and mould. Water pooled on the floor in various places, and I had to watch my step. The replica needed a bit of maintenance of its own, and I wondered how different its conditions were than the original. (The replica was removed from the water a year or so after my visit for much-needed restoration.) Before me, rows of rough pine bunk beds were stacked three and four beds high, with just two feet between tiers. Puke and latrine buckets were set up at each corner. Canvas and blankets partitioned areas from one another, but they would have offered little privacy.

I couldn't imagine staying down there another minute, and the very idea of my forebears living this way for weeks was horrifying. I pictured the chaos and imagined the scents and sounds of this small space packed to capacity with starving, violently ill passengers and screaming children. It would have been a living hell with seemingly no end in sight.

Back up on deck, I took a deep, grateful breath of fresh air. I could still taste the mould. I walked back to my car, taking note of the scenery around me in the bustling small town of Pictou and its historic waterfront. It looked nothing like it would have 245 years earlier.

The immigrants had disembarked up the coast a bit at a place called Brown's Point. There's a painting in the Quay dated 1773 that shows two rowboats heading toward a partially cleared lot with one small house on the hill surrounded by tree stumps. Apparently, as those boats rowed the short distance from the *Hector* to shore with its weary passengers, the men wore their Scottish kilts for the occasion and the bagpiper played.

The land of Pictou was not what was promised by the recruiters back in Scotland. Aside from a few log houses and a store—set up by some American settler families—the land appeared to the newcomers as wilderness. It was dense forest as far as the eye could see. The Scottish newcomers were not given the coastal land they'd been pledged, but uncleared plots inland. It was described in Donald MacKay's book, *Scotland Farewell: The People of the Hector* (1980), as "a primeval forest thick with deadfalls, silent with dark and gloomy groves of pine which soared 200 feet to shut out any light."

There were also few available provisions, and the Highlanders were left to mostly fend for themselves. Having arrived in September, it was too late to plant crops. Some families almost starved during their first winter.

Many more ships followed the *Hector* across the Atlantic. By 1849, 120 ships had landed in Pictou, bringing 9,701 people, almost all Scottish. By 1879, there were some English names in the towns, but the Scots outnumbered the others three to one. The majority of those who arrived from Scotland stayed in the area, or at least in Nova Scotia. It might have been because that was the easier option, or maybe they felt it resembled their homeland. Especially the island of Cape Breton on the eastern coast of Nova Scotia, which offers lush green mountains and high cliffs overlooking the sea. Although the Pictou settlement was small in the early days, towns were starting to form in other areas of the province, including nearby Truro. And the city of Halifax that had been founded by European settlers in 1749, was booming.

The Mi'kmaw people lived in the area and co-existed peacefully with the new settlers, despite an initial fear brought on by the sound of the bagpipes, which legend claims frightened the Mi'kmaq so much that they fled into the woods and stayed there for months, as noted in James M. Cameron's *Pictou County's History* (1972). In many cases, the Mi'kmaq helped the new settlers, teaching them basic survival skills.

When I was a kid, a friend's mom played the bagpipes. The piercing sound echoed through every room of their house, even though Mrs. MacLellan practised outside. It was unavoidable. Though she played well, I wasn't used to the powerful and haunting sound. And when she'd hit a wrong note, it was impossible not to cringe. It's still common to hear bagpipers at community events in Pictou County and to see people wearing kilts at weddings, but that's about the extent of my Scottish cultural experiences. The plaid pattern of the Murray tartan that I had viewed at the interpretive centre was completely unfamiliar to me. I wonder how long those early Scottish settlers wore their tartan colours after arriving in Nova Scotia? And at what point did they start to lose interest in this tradition?

Heritage still plays a role in the lives of some Scottish settler descendants. For example, Gaelic is still spoken by about 1,300 Nova Scotians. The only other place the language is spoken in any significant number is Scotland, with fewer than 60,000 people fluent.

Even surrounded by Scottish descendants, cultural traditions have played no part in my life. I've never taken a highland dance class or watched a Highland Games or celebrated Robbie Burns Day (although eating baked haggis followed by shots of whisky does sound like something I'd be into trying at least once).

Because my grandmother had six sisters and just one brother, the Murray name was mostly lost to us. But Aunt Doris, who was practically raised by her Murray grandparents, wanted to keep the name in the family and gave her only son the first name of Murray. Years ago, she visited Blair Castle, the ancestral home of Clan Murray. She showed me pictures of a beautiful white fortress surrounded by mountains in Perthshire, Scotland. The elaborate thirty-room castle is impressive, with its grand entrance hall, tapestry room, and ballroom. Before seeing her pictures, I had no idea such a place even existed. It seemed a world and time away, but if you were to trace my family tree back a few centuries, it would eventually lead to that castle.

I casually mentioned to my father one day that I was going to start looking into the genealogy of my mother's family, the Murrays.

"Hold off on your research," he said, adding that he might know a guy who could help.

My father always knows someone. He and my brother, Kevin, run a small business in New Glasgow—a home heating fuel company that has been in the McKay family since 1928—and there are times when I'm pretty sure he knows every single person in town.

A few weeks later, my father called me with an update. A man named Corey Hartling, who researched local history as a hobby, had compiled hundreds of years' worth of Murray family facts into what my father referred to as a "book" and dropped it off for me. Much of it was research he had completed for other Murray families over the years—people I didn't know—but he also added facts and information that would address my specific research questions.

"Did he find the connection between us and the quintuplets' family?" I asked. I had questioned Grammie many times on the subject, but she always said that although she knew we were related to the babies, she had no idea how.

"I didn't have time to sort through it all," my father admitted. This was my mother's family after all, not his, but he was a bit of a local history buff himself. "You'll have to ask your brother. He took it and is trying to figure it out."

This surprised me, as my brother had never expressed any interest in the old family story.

New Glasgow, where my father and brother live, is an hour-and-a-half drive from my home in Halifax. I couldn't wait any longer for this first crumb to get me started, and I drove there the following afternoon.

I had assumed when my father called the research a "book," he had misspoken. I expected him to pass along a thin file folder with some hand-drawn family names, most likely sketched into the likeness of a giant tree. This wasn't the case.

When I met up with Kevin at his workplace, he handed over an inch-and-a-half–thick, coil bound "book"—and it couldn't be described as anything else. I was in awe at how much material had been gifted to me.

On the front was a photocopied picture of the quintuplets with the title *The Murray Quintuplets and Their Descendants*. This was inaccurate, as the quintuplets lived only a few days and had no direct descendants, but it was clear what the local historian who compiled it meant: the people who came before and after. The book was a gold mine of information. Inside were pages upon pages of Murray family details dating back to the late 1700s. In addition to the family breakdowns, there were copies of marriage certificates, obituaries, newspaper articles, and old census records. It was far more than I had hoped for.

Kevin had already gone through some of it and added paperclips to the tops of the pages he thought I would find helpful.

"I didn't know you were interested in this stuff," I said to him.

"I'm interested," he said, giving me a smile and a look, a reminder that the story didn't belong to me alone.

Kevin flipped the book open to his first marked page.

There it was: a name, and a clear connection to the Murray quints. The name was Hector Murray, and he would have been my great-great-great-great-grandfather. I also had a piece of information that contradicted what I'd always believed about my Murray family origins in Nova Scotia. I'd been told my Murray forebears had arrived on the *Hector*, but thanks to the work of my father's local historian friend, I discovered that wasn't so.

The *Hector* voyage was notable because it was the first, but dozens of ships followed soon after. Each successfully making the same hazardous transatlantic journey and bringing over hundreds of Scottish families. Many of those later arrivals had connections to the *Hector* settlers—they were their parents, children, cousins, neighbours, and friends. My direct Murray ancestors—including the forebears of the quintuplets—arrived on one of those other ships, the name and travel date are unknown. (However, both my McKay and Patterson ancestors on my father's side did arrive on the *Hector*!)

Hector Murray (no connection to the ship's name) had followed his cousin Walter to Nova Scotia; Walter had travelled on the *Hector* years before. Hector—the man, not the ship—and his family were from Sutherlandshire, Scotland. Sutherlandshire, more commonly known as Sutherland, is a county in the north of Scotland. Interestingly, the area was also the homeland of Clan MacKay, and the two families—my maternal and paternal ancestors—were said to be mortal enemies.

It's from this point that the branches of my Murray family tree, as well as the quintuplets' family, began to grow in Nova Scotia.

When Hector's family arrived in Nova Scotia, he was offered a plot of land in the community of Little Harbour. The land was likely granted to him for free, as it was part of planned colonization by Europeans who were setting up settlements in the area.

The small community was made up of homes and farms built around the inner harbours and facing the Northumberland Strait. Among Hector's five children on the long journey were sons Thomas and James, who were six and three at the time. When the young Scottish-born brothers grew up, they both married women who were also Scottish immigrants. Thomas married Christina Fraser and they moved to the community of Merigomish, where they had one son, Adam (the father of the quintuplets), born in 1822. James and his wife, Johanna Ross, had four children, including my great-great-grandfather John, born in 1840.

The quints' father, Adam, and my great-great-grandfather John were first cousins. This was the connection.

When Adam Murray was eighteen, he married Sarah Green. The couple had two sons together (Duncan in 1841 and Thomas in 1850). Sarah died unexpectedly at the age of twenty-six, leaving Adam a widower. In June 1867, when Adam was forty-four, he married again. His new bride was nineteen-year-old Maria (pronounced Ma-rye-ah) Rankin from Little Harbour. Maria grew up on Roy Island, just past what is now Melmerby Beach Provincial Park.

An older man marrying a teenage girl was more common in the nineteenth century than it is today, but I couldn't help but wonder about the circumstances of such a marriage. How did Adam and Maria meet? Was it something the families arranged? Maria was in fact seven years younger than Adam's eldest son, and just two years older than his youngest. Perhaps it was more an arrangement of convenience and circumstance?

Adam was an experienced farmer, having grown up on a farm in Merigomish, and he and some cousins had an opportunity to purchase, or were perhaps granted, land of their own in the late 1860s or early 1870s. In an illustrated historical atlas of Pictou County from 1879, a map of Little Egypt shows a cluster of farm properties titled: "The Murray Farm Settlement." The land was divided up among Adam (two hundred acres); his cousin, my great-great-grandfather, John (one hundred acres); John's brother Hector (two hundred acres), and two other men who I assume were cousins, George (two hundred acres), and David (one hundred acres). (It's sometimes difficult to navigate the family tree, as there are multiple relatives with the same first name across generations and families. For example, there are a number of Thomases, Johns, Jims, Georges, Christines, and Dorises.) It's not known why the other Murray lands were never developed or lived on, but the only two properties with homes and farms were John's and Adam's sharing the eight hundred acres. Because the land was so vast, the homes were not within sight of one another, but far across the fields on opposite sides.

In the eighteenth and early nineteenth centuries, it was typical for people to have large families. As fatal childhood illness was common, couples tended to have as many children as they could to ensure the survival of the family line. And if you lived on a farm, more children meant additional hands for working.

Adam and Maria began to grow their family immediately, with a child born almost every year during the early years of their marriage.

In 1875, tragedy struck their little home. Adam and Maria lost three young children to diphtheria (a potentially deadly bacterial infection causing a thick greyish coating in the back of the throat, making it difficult to breathe and swallow): George, five; Margaret Jane, three and a half; and Elizabeth, just nine months. There would have been no money for a cemetery burial, and it was common practice at the time for children to be buried on a family's property. Were they buried in the woods behind the farm in unmarked graves? No one knows for sure, but I couldn't find a marked grave in any local cemetery.

Five years later, in February 1880, when the quintuplets were born, the couple had five young children at home, who ranged in age from three to thirteen. Newspaper accounts of the quintuplets' births suggested there were already seven children in the household. It is possible that Adam's two older sons were living in the house, or they may have been residing nearby and counted in this number.

Armed with this probable information about the births and deaths of family members, I began to paint a picture of life in the little Murray farmhouse.

LITTLE EGYPT, 1880: THE DOCTOR ARRIVES

The drive by horse and sleigh from the Murray settlement to Dr. William Fraser Downie's home on Provost Street in New Glasgow was about four miles. "Downie" wasn't part of the doctor's actual name but added because he was one of the Frasers who lived "down the hill." There were many, many Fraser families in the town, and people often gave them extra, descriptive names to distinguish one family from another.

Being awakened in the middle of the night to attend to a patient was not unusual for Dr. Fraser, as it came with the job of a small-town physician. So, when the messenger arrived, he immediately got out of bed and hitched up his own horse and sleigh.

When something was unique about a birth, such as twins—which he may have thought was the case with Mrs. Murray—he sometimes brought along help. (He may also have known there were five babies at this point; it's impossible to know.) On his way to the farm, he picked up James Jackson, the local druggist, who was considered a prominent local citizen. (This makes particular sense if all five babies had been born by the time the doctor was sent for.)

The ride was brisk along the lonely, dark country roads. Snow fell around them. They travelled through the burgeoning little town of North New Glasgow to the Glenfalloch Road, then to the remote Murray Lane that led to the farm settlement in Little Egypt. The drive took about an hour.

Dr. Fraser was a respected doctor with sixteen years of experience under his belt. He had graduated at the top of his class of five hundred students from Glasgow University in Scotland. His specialty was surgery (as noted in Clyde F. Macdonald's *Notable Events in Pictou County*).

As Dr. Fraser passed Elizabeth and John Murray's house the morning of February 15, 1880, the sun was inching its way into the eastern sky. The land and fields were still dark ahead of him, shadowed by the rolling hills and surrounding trees. On such a morning, the extreme cold would make fingers go numb inside thick mittens and force anyone to pull their coat just a little tighter.

Light from a kerosene lamp flickered through the windows of Adam and Maria's modest home, creating a beacon for Dr. Fraser as he approached. He had been to the Murray settlement on other occasions. He may even have been there when Adam and Maria's children were sick with diphtheria in the spring five years earlier. He was, perhaps, thinking about just that tragedy as his sleigh neared the farm. The illness had affected many in the county, but the loss of life was felt especially hard when it was children.

One of the Murray men was waiting anxiously in the yard as the doctor's sleigh approached. Dr. Fraser's horse was unhooked and taken into the barn, allowing the doctor and the pharmacist to rush in. They understood the urgency.

The wood stove was pumping out heat in the small farmhouse, but the kitchen was drafty. There were kerosene lamps burning but not enough, and the house was dark—so much so that the doctor could barely make out Maria's form in the bed. There was little in the way of furnishings. What the family had was old and worn. The kitchen was unkempt and in need of a good cleaning. It was very early in the morning, and although there were chores to be done, the children were distracted by the excitement in the house.

Elizabeth or one of the children would have been quick to inform the doctor there wasn't one new baby, but five (if he didn't already know).

The family was in a state of shock and excitement. How could this happen? They looked to the doctor for answers, but in all his years, Dr. Fraser had never seen or even heard of such a birth. Twins, yes. Quintuplets, never.

He took over for Elizabeth, who was feeling overwhelmed and exhausted, and began examining the infants. There were three girls and two boys. All were tiny but otherwise perfect in every way. Each had ten fingers and ten toes, and a tiny flawless face. They were pale and not as pink as they should be. He checked each baby for a heartbeat—it was there, but low. Their pulses were also low, and their breathing shallow.

Although Adam Murray may have been worrying about how he would feed five extra mouths, there were bigger problems at hand. Dr. Fraser, James Jackson, and Elizabeth Murray would have been concerned about keeping the babies alive. Clearly Maria would not have enough milk to feed five newborns. They would need to use a dropper for now and put word out immediately to find a wet nurse. Plus, there was their diminutive size. Dr. Fraser might also have been worrying about infection setting in, which was sometimes a cause of infant death at that time. The Murray house was not a sterile environment. Some of the babies were, at that moment, wrapped in dusty window blinds.

He knew that all they could do was keep the infants adequately warm—and hope and pray.

Word of the unusual birth spread quickly. Elizabeth probably sent Tom home to gather more blankets and supplies, and to tell the family the news. They, in turn, told other neighbours in Little Egypt. Soon, the story of Maria Murray's five babies reached the town, and from there, the telegraph service, and then, the world.

CHAPTER 3:

THE OTHER MURRAY FARM IN LITTLE EGYPT

When I was nine, I asked my grandmother to take me to see the land that was once the old Murray farm. She said she knew exactly where the quintuplets' house had been and promised to show me the precise spot.

On the day of our excursion, she picked up my brother and me in her shiny new white Toyota Tercel. I'm certain her car was new, not because it made an impression on me but because she always had a new car, never keeping a vehicle longer than a year. Her cars were usually white, and the make was always Toyota. Since she was the dealership's best customer, they would often buy her extravagant Christmas presents like expensive watches or electronics that she didn't understand how to use. At her funeral, decades later, Toyota sent the biggest flower arrangement available.

Upon her arrival at our house that morning, Grammie parked as close to the front door as possible and beeped her horn. This was how she typically visited. She would park and beep, and we would come out and sit in the car with her for a short visit, then we would get out and she would drive off. She only came into the house when she was there for her weekly curler set, which my mother, a hairdresser, did for her every Thursday in the one-room hair salon in our basement.

The drive from my home to Little Egypt took about fifteen minutes, travelling along narrow, twisty country roads. Sometimes I'd feel carsick in the back seat but not that day. I was too excited. The Murray property was easy to spot, as it was a large open field that seemed to go on forever—it was the only place like it along the road. I felt anticipation as Grammie slowly pulled the car onto the wildly overgrown driveway. The ride was bumpy, and she manoeuvred slowly around the deep potholes and tall weeds. At the time of this visit, the land belonged to my Aunt Ginger, my mother's older sister, and her husband. They didn't live there—no one did—and the fields were empty. My uncle used the land to train his Labrador retrievers and kept the property clear of brush and trees. My grandmother said it looked almost as she remembered it when she was young; it was just missing the old farmhouse and barns—and, of course, the people. (It looks nothing like that now, as new families have built massive homes on the property, making the land their own. I prefer to remember it as it was the day I visited as a little girl: wild, peaceful, and full of mystery.)

My grandmother stopped the car midway along the gently sloping field near the visible ruins of an old house.

"This was it," I thought, gazing out the rolled-down window from the back seat of the car. The old stone foundation was visible from the road, and I had passed it hundreds of times on the way to and from Grammie's house. Since hearing the story of the quintuplets, I always made a point of staring intently at the old ruins when we drove by, trying to spot some sort of clue. Now, I was actually there and took in every detail. I could clearly make out where each of the four walls once stood. The back wall was the highest, climbing up out of the embankment. A few trees were growing in amongst the stones. Some were tall, having been there a very long time. I tried to imagine the layout of the home. Where was the kitchen? The bedroom? The living room?

I thought it was the most magical place on earth. This was where the five babies were born. It was in that very basement—which was clearly visible to me—that they were once buried. This was where our special, wonderful family story had taken place.

"This isn't it," my grandmother announced, bursting my bubble. "This was where *our* farm once stood."

"There were *two* Murray farms?" I asked.

"Yes. The other Murray farm was way up there." She pointed up the hill and over to the left. "We'll have to walk."

It was early summer, and the hay was already tall and green and golden. I was wearing flip-flops, and water squished between my toes when I got out of the car. Grammie wore an impractical form of footwear, a dress shoe with a closed toe and a small heel. She owned nothing suitable for a field trip of this sort. She hiked her calf-length, thin cotton dress up above her knees and led the way. We walked northeast on uneven ground. Any paths that linked the two Murray farm properties were long overgrown. The tall grass tickled and scratched my bare legs. My brother—who I had already forgotten was even with us—lost interest in our quest and ran back to the ruins of the house near the car to climb one of the trees.

The walk took longer than I expected, given what looked to be a relatively short distance. My grandmother was in her mid-sixties and in good health, but the extra weight she carried was a burden. She complained about having bad legs. Sweat drew lines in her bright pink blush. She wiped it away with the tissue she kept in her bra.

After about fifteen minutes of walking, she stopped a few feet from the woods.

"It's too wet," she said. "The other Murray house was in there." There was no uncertainty in her voice. She knew the house. She had been in it as a child. "It was right in there." She pointed and jiggled her finger toward the thick dense greenery. The trees and brush ahead of us were so thick the light of day didn't shine through.

"These trees weren't here back then," she added. "This was all farmland, clear as you could see."

"Can't we try to go in closer?" I begged.

"You go ahead," she said.

I was keen to venture in and explore on my own, but as I neared the edge of the woods, my already wet feet became submerged in a bog. I was soaked up to my knees.

"I'll take you back another day," she promised.

She never did.

The idea of a property that is home to generations of family members is something foreign to most people these days. Today, the average person moves eleven times in their lifetime. I have already lived in fifteen different places, and I can certainly see myself moving again.

Our Murray farm, which originally belonged to my great-great-grandparents, John and Elizabeth Murray, was a true family

A family painting of John and Elizabeth Murray's farm.

home. When my grandmother, my mother, and her sisters talked about things that happened "out on the farm," I could tell it wasn't just a place to them, it was a way of life. It was the family homestead that connected them. Family members drifted in and out over the years, but someone always had to be working the land and the job didn't fall to any one person. Siblings moved away and came back. They took turns spending their weekends there. They left to have families, and when their children were grown, they returned in their senior years.

Like a fine-tuned family business, the farm served my Murray ancestors well.

When Adam Murray, the father of the quintuplets who lived on the neighbouring Murray land, died in 1908, none of his children stayed on to run their family farm, and the home and barns eventually fell to ruin. The property was abandoned. Yet John and Elizabeth's farm—our family property—remained a staple landmark on the Little Egypt Road, as my great-great-aunts and uncles and their children continued the farming traditions for generations. I believe this is why the story stayed with our family. It stayed on that land.

As the decades went by and the faces on our Murray farm changed, times also changed in the town around them. The town grew. Industry boomed. Progress was happening everywhere. Yet, at the Murray farmhouse, things stayed the same. The farm never had electricity or indoor plumbing. It never had a television set or a telephone. The family never relied on grocery stores; they lived off the vegetables, fruit, meat, and wheat they took from the land. They used their horse and wagon long after the motorized car was invented. This was all by choice, not necessity. The family was hard-working and had money—which was kept, as Murray family rumours had it, hidden in the walls of the house—but they chose to live a simple life. It was an old-style working farm until the late 1950s, when John's eleven children became too old to work it.

If you were to ask anyone from the area today if they knew the location of the Murray quintuplets' family farmhouse, most would probably say no. The few who said yes would likely point to where my ancestor's farm once stood and not the property where Adam and Maria raised their family. That land has long been hidden from view, and very few people today know a second Murray farm ever existed.

I was fascinated with the Murray property not only because it had a tangible connection to the quintuplets, but also because the land was once home to generations of my ancestors—most of whom are now almost completely forgotten. Who were the Murrays? What did they look like? What were they like? I wanted to find out.

Although I could no longer see our family's farmhouse, I could envision where it once stood. I could see the same footprint of land; these were the same fields that once grew carrots, lettuce, potatoes, and apples that fed my family before me. It housed their horses and chickens and pets. Somewhere on that land were the remnants of the old well where they got their water from an underground stream that still flows. I felt a connection to it.

Before I started my family research for this book, I knew very little about the Murray farm or its inhabitants. As my grandmother and all seven of her siblings died years ago—the last sister passed away in 2011 at age ninety-six—I now had to rely on my mother and her sisters to share their family stories with me.

I arranged to meet my Aunt Doris one afternoon at her cottage. Doris is my mother's oldest sister on her mother's side (my grandfather also had two daughters from a previous marriage), and although she was in her early eighties at the time, she had a sort of timeless appearance and way about her, hardly seeming to age over the years I've known her. All my mother's sisters and their cousins of that same generation are like that, as were the Murray sisters before them—most of whom lived long healthy lives well into their late eighties and nineties.

Doris's cottage is in Black Point, which is about a ten-minute drive from Little Egypt Road. Her place is close to my own cottage, where my husband, children, and I spend our summers. We're on the ocean side of Black Point—a long jut of land that supposedly got its name from a forest fire that blackened all the trees centuries ago—and Doris is on the back inner harbour, which is calm and sheltered, much like a lake.

When I asked if I could stop by to talk about the quintuplets and her years on the farm, Doris warned me, "I don't know much." I knew otherwise. If anyone alive today knew anything, it was her.

The day was cool and cloudy. My mother and my eleven-year-old niece Casey came along with me. Casey, unlike my own kids, was interested in the story of the quintuplets. When I talk about the old family stories with my children, their eyes glaze over. I'm not sure if it's a general lack of interest in history, or just that I've mentioned the quintuplets' story too many times. Perhaps Casey will be the keeper of these memories for future generations. When I was young, I was always keen to learn new things—especially about our past—and I love that my niece holds a similar spark of curiosity.

Doris arrived at the cottage just minutes before we did. She no longer stays overnight at the shore, not since her husband Frank passed away a year earlier. Cancer caught them by surprise and took him quickly. Now, she drives to the cottage from her house in town.

"Are you cold?" she asked when we came in. "Should I turn on the heat?"

"No, it's fine," I said. The cottage wasn't warm, but it wasn't exactly cold either. She offered to make tea but then realized there was no milk.

The cottage is an open concept design, with a single room for the kitchen and living space. She had a line of big chairs set up to face the water through the front windows. The place smelled clean but closed-up. Unused. The four of us sat spread out around the spacious room. The view through her front window was breathtaking, even with the grey sky. The water was still, and her front yard was neat and green. A large blue heron stood off in the distance, graceful and static.

Although I hadn't spent much time at Doris's cottage growing up, as I looked through her front window I was overwhelmed with a sense of nostalgia. I remembered a visit when I was young. My cousins and I discovered a wild raspberry bush in the yard—something I'd never seen before or since. We stood at it, picking and eating, for hours.

I was pleased that my research had provided a reason for me to spend time with my aunt. Ideally, I shouldn't need a purpose to connect with family, but sometimes one is necessary. Not everyone is good at keeping in touch. There's an anonymous quote that resonates: "Families are like branches on a tree. We grow in different directions, yet our roots remain as one." Regardless of how frequently we visit or communicate, we share a vital connection with our relatives: DNA. It bonds us. My ancestors are not just names in a story; they also constitute my physical history. With this book, I aimed to revisit the past I knew, discover the one I didn't, and strengthen my ties with my family in the present.

As I sat next to Doris on her firm two-seat sofa, I couldn't help but think of my grandmother. When I looked at my aunt, I saw Grammie. Her soft white hair and flawless pale skin seemed like an echo of the past. I would give anything to see my grandmother again.

I took out my little recorder, turned it on, and set it on the table in front of us.

"Let's start with the Murray farm," I said. "Can you describe it to me?"

"Our farm? You know there were two."

"Yes, I know," I said.

She assumed I thought what everyone else thought: that the babies were born on our property.

"I'm including the story of our farm in my book," I told her.

She nodded, as if in agreement that we were part of the story too.

"Our property was made up of the main farmhouse, plus three barns," she began. "One barn was used as a blacksmith shop, where the men would shoe the horses and make or fix any other metal items they needed on the farm. The second barn, located near the pasture, was for the horses and cows. And the smallest barn, which was close to the house, was for the chickens and pigs. There was also an icehouse, where they stored food throughout the year, and a four-seater outhouse. It was always very clean," Doris noted. "They used lime to control the smell and the flies."

I was more interested in the four seats.

"Did the family all go to the bathroom at the same time?" I asked.

She actually had no idea why there were four seats, but I later found out outhouse seats were constructed with different-sized holes for the children, so the younger kids didn't fall through the adult-sized openings. Who knew this inquiry into my family's story would yield such additional fascinating information?

Doris went on to tell me that when she was young, an assortment of John and Elizabeth's children—Doris's great-aunts and -uncles—all lived on the farm. "Each person had a role," she said. The men tended the animals and the land; the women cooked and cleaned and looked after the household. Everyone would rise with the sun and retire at dusk. They worked hard and ended their days exhausted. I wondered if their days felt rewarding. It isn't an existence I can imagine, but it sounds like a peaceful life.

"The farmhouse itself was white with a little covered porch and a black roof. When you first went in the back door—which was the door everyone used, so as not to soil the front room floors with dirty shoes and boots—you were in the main pantry, with a smaller second pantry off to the side," said Doris. "The pantry always had cookies in cans that were sealed tight to keep the mice out. Through the pantry was the kitchen, which had a big square sink and water pump that needed constant priming. There was a wood stove in the centre of the kitchen with a chair beside it. That chair was where Aunt Sarah always sat in the winter to keep warm."

Sarah was her grandfather's sister, who lived almost her entire life on the farm. She had an intellectual disability and was considered "simple" in those times, with no actual diagnosis ever noted or probably known.

As Doris described the farmhouse in detail, I could picture it vividly. I could even imagine the smell of the wood fire burning and the pies cooking in the oven, the hardworking, busy family going about their daily lives with determination, wearing exceptionally clean farm clothes (they were Murrays, after all).

"The stairs were right there in front of the main door, and the formal dining room was on the left and the parlour on the right," she said, gesturing with her hands.

Behind the parlour was where her Uncle Jim slept. Sarah and Libby (her grandfather's other sister) had little rooms off the dining room. The family worked hard and had money, and their furniture was beautiful and expensive. There was a round dark oak dining room table, a pump organ, and pretty pink sofas in the living room. (Almost everything was lost when the house burned in the 1960s. One of the few known remaining artifacts is the ornate parlour mirror that currently hangs in Doris's entryway in New Glasgow.)

The upstairs of the farmhouse was a place the children were not allowed to venture when Doris and her sisters were young. It was mostly empty bedrooms that were drafty and cold and generally unused. The only person who slept up there was her Uncle Geordie, who didn't seem to be remembered fondly by anyone and was most commonly described as "a cranky old drunk."

"I was upstairs only one time," Doris told me. It was when she and her sister Ginger, who was two years younger than her, were invited for a sleepover as kids. "We were in one of the old bedrooms, and the beds were tick mattresses," she said—old-style beds made from a coarse cotton material and filled with straw. Her great-aunts and -uncles had new mattresses at that point, but these were the old mattresses from when they were children.

"The straw kept sticking in us and we kept laughing, and Geordie yelled at us all night to be quiet," said Doris.

When Geordie and his siblings were growing up in that same house, the sound of children would have been common.

In 1880, the year the quintuplets were born, the little upstairs bedrooms in our Murray farmhouse were full. There were seven children then—Ann, the oldest at twelve; Thomas, eleven; Johanna, eight; Elizabeth (Libby), six; James (Jim), five; Andrew (my grandfather), three; and George (Geordie), one. The older kids slept on the upper level and the younger kids slept downstairs with their parents.

I asked Doris what she knew about Adam and Maria's farmhouse. She said it was there in the woods when she was very little, but she was never inside. Her relatives described it to her as a simple house with a big wood stove in the kitchen. There was an upstairs with little bedrooms, and a small parlour off the kitchen.

Doris remembers a time when she was out in the field as a teenager and came upon the foundation of an old house. Beside the foundation was a tree with one russet apple on it.

"I remember I picked the apple and took it home to show Grandpa," she said. "He told me: 'That was the old Adam Murray farm. Adam Murray had a russet apple tree there by the house.'"

I felt like I had stumbled upon an important detail here. It brought me closer to the lost house, and the lost story. I hadn't seen the exact spot, but Doris had. I was determined to keep searching.

The Murray farms were located in a part of the county known as Glenfalloch or Hillside on maps, but was—and still is—most commonly referred to as Little Egypt by the locals. It's a name I always felt was unusual and curious. There is no obvious connection with the country of Egypt—it couldn't look more different, with its dense green fir trees—and no one knows exactly why the early settlers named it this. Southern Illinois, for example, is often referred to as Little Egypt because its pioneers thought it resembled the Nile, with its low-lying landscape, fertile land, and frequent flooding from localized rivers. The best explanation I can find for the use of "Egypt" in this case is a slang term meaning "the middle of nowhere" or "a place that's far away and difficult to get to." This is an apt description, as the nearest town at that time, New Glasgow, was more than four miles away and required travel on back country roads.

When John and Adam first built their farms, theirs were two of only a few in Little Egypt. Today, there are certainly more than a handful of homes, but the area is still sparsely populated. Little Egypt isn't a town or even a community, it's just a place. It's a connector road that runs from Trenton to Little Harbour. The two-and-a-half-mile stretch is peppered with mostly older homes at one end and larger, newer homes at the other. There are a few semi-retired farm properties in the middle. The road is winding. Vehicles drive too fast.

I know Little Egypt Road well. Not only did I visit my grandmother there, but I have memories of my own. I learned how to drive on that road in Grammie's Toyota Tercel, which was considerably smaller and easier to manoeuvre than my parents' Oldsmobile.

I went to elementary school with a kid from Little Egypt. In high school, I dated a boy who lived just a ten-minute walk from the Murray farm property. It is also the road we currently drive to get to and from our cottage in nearby Black Point.

The road itself has changed a great deal since 1880. Then, the nearby town of Trenton didn't even exist (it was known as North New Glasgow), and the Glenfalloch Road that ran through the area was well-used by people on their way to the train stations in Pictou Landing or the community of Woodburn.

Along the Little Egypt Road today, side roads that once veered off the main road no longer exist. One such road was called the Murray Road or "the crossroad." Instead of going straight to the next community of Little Harbour, the Little Egypt Road forked, and people could take one of two paths: the main road that still exists today or "the crossroad," which took you through to the Murray farm settlement.

Although this second thoroughfare is no longer used in any capacity, my mother remembers it from when she was a child. But even then, in the late 1950s, it was used far less than it had been at the turn of the century. It was desolate and neglected.

"I remember walking that road as a young child," my mother told me. "I would leave my house near Trenton and head out to the farm. Dad used to help my great-uncles (John and Elizabeth Murray's sons) on weekends, and that would be my excuse to visit. It was about an hour away. I'd walk all by myself, never seeing anyone go by. It was scary, actually, as there were no houses along the way. I would run as fast as I could. It was a road you took during the day, but never at night."

I asked her to help me find it. Like deserted homes and buildings, abandoned roads represent a time before. A lifetime forgotten. I find them fascinating. And I'm not alone. I'm a member of a Facebook group called Abandoned Roads of Nova Scotia, which, at the time of publishing, had more than twenty-eight thousand members. There are unused roads crisscrossing the entire province, and most people don't even know they're there. I'm drawn to the pictures people post of overgrown roads, abandoned cars and homes, forgotten lakes, and old bridges. It reaffirms my predilection for the slightly macabre, the abandoned, the obscure—and the untold stories they carry.

My mother was keen to accompany me on this drive down memory lane. We set out one Sunday morning in fall 2018. But what seemed a sure thing in her memory was less solid in practice. She slowed the car several times to find what she thought might be the right road. The land looked completely different, she told me. Time had changed everything around us. She eventually turned down a road called Cairo Lane; another mysterious connection to Egypt, I noted. It came to a dead end quickly and she pulled over to the side. Straight ahead of us lay a muddy path—the remnants of the road we were looking for. It appeared passable only by all-terrain vehicle or by walking with gear that included knee-high rubber boots. It was late fall, and the surrounding trees were mostly bare. The ground was yellow with freshly fallen leaves.

"I think this was where it started," she said, pointing. "This should meet up again a little further down." She turned her SUV around and drove back out onto Little Egypt Road. The next turnoff we came to was Old Glenfalloch Road, which is still used as a secondary country road today. On Google maps, you can see it goes for miles and miles. Most of it has never been paved. We didn't venture far—less than a minute—before she stopped in the middle of the road again. There were a few driveways that led to houses we couldn't see, but the road was quiet. There was no risk of traffic.

"This is where 'the crossroads' came from Cairo Lane," she said, pointing to a clear path on her right, "and then it continued across here and went along to the farm." Her finger travelled from one side of the road to the other. What remained of the old Murray Road was then visible to me on both sides.

It was late morning, yet despite the shining sun, the tree-lined path looked as if dusk had already fallen, with densely crowded branches of multicoloured leaves stretching to meet overhead. Young trees sprouted at the path's edges. A hundred and thirty years before, or even sixty, it might have been wide enough for a horse and wagon, but today it's a narrow one-way lane. Although no one travels this path these days, it was the road four generations of my family used regularly. It passed right in front of my great-great-grandparents' farmhouse and the farm's blacksmith shop and barns. It's also the road that once led to Adam and Maria Murray's farm.

"At one time, mayflowers grew in the woods alongside this old road," my mother said.

"Really?" I had never heard this before. I wondered if this was where my grandmother was first introduced to the flower that would become her lifelong obsession.

The mayflower, a wild trailing pink-and-white flowering plant, is the provincial flower of Nova Scotia. That doesn't mean it's found in abundance around the province. In season in May, the flowers are surprisingly difficult to find. Few Nova Scotians have probably even seen them, unless, of course, they knew my grandmother.

Grammie would track down mayflowers all over Pictou County each spring. Even in her late seventies, she and her sister Christine, known to the family as "Teenie," could be spotted on the side of the highway kneeling in some ditch, or out on a back road, gathering and filling her car's trunk with the sweet-smelling flowers. She would then take her treasures home, clean them, bundle them in little glasses of water, and put them in her fridge. When we went to visit her, or if we were summoned to her house for the purpose of receiving our annual mayflowers, we left with a small bouquet. She would wrap the roots in a damp paper towel for transport.

Because the flower is considered endangered today, if you find some, you are encouraged to leave them, or at least the root, so they can come back again the following year. I can't help but wonder whether Grammie and Teenie's ravaging of the province's woods each spring is why the flowers are so rare today.

"We should come out here sometime and look for mayflowers," I said to my mother. I have no idea where else they might be located. I once thought I could smell them in the wind at our cottage and searched the nearby woods, but I had no luck finding any. I've never seen them growing wild anywhere.

My mother shrugged. It was her mother's thing, not hers. And not really mine. As much as I would love to have a bouquet for my table, the tradition of yearly bunches of mayflowers ended when my grandmother passed away thirteen years before.

My mother and I sat in the SUV in the middle of the road for a few minutes. I thought about going out for a closer look at "the crossroads," but when I opened the door a dog started barking hysterically from some unseen property. Even though it wasn't private land, it felt like we were somewhere we no longer belonged. I closed the door.

ANNIE MARGARET (MURRAY) (BROOKS) BROWN

When I was a teenager, I once told my mother I thought my grandmother's life would make a great book. She was quick to shoot down the idea.

"She would be horrified if anyone knew her secrets," my mother said.

Annie Margaret Brown was a different sort of person, unlike the typical doting, nurturing, cookie-baking grandmother you might have in mind. She lived alone in a home she owned, had a valid driver's license (which was a bit rare for a woman her age in the late 1970s and early '80s), and loved her independence. She had strong opinions and would always tell you exactly what she thought.

As a teenager, I feared what she might say to my friends when she stopped by our house to visit. On more than one occasion, she told a friend they appeared to have gained weight since the last time she'd seen them. Grammie was raised at a time when it was still common and acceptable to notice and comment on a person's body—especially a woman's body—and she was not one for filtering her thoughts before she spoke them.

Grammie never travelled, except around the province, and loved the comfort of her tiny, four-room house. She loved her family in short visits, but didn't always enjoy the company of others.

She was nothing like my grandmother on my father's side, whose home was always lively. I was at my McKay grandparents' house almost daily as a child. Whenever I walked in, their friendly black poodle, Nicky, would greet me, as would the smell of whatever my grandmother was cooking in the kitchen. Theirs was a home filled with people and noise and life, where Grammie Brown's house was welcoming, but quiet, except for the whisper of her little black-and-white TV.

Grammie wasn't into material things. Her home was sparsely decorated; there was never clutter. This was, in part, because she gave everything away. She was incredibly kind. When we were kids, we would bring her a Christmas present on Christmas Eve, and she would open it right then, which always bothered me because I thought she should wait until morning like the rest of us. She would smile and thank us, and in return she would give us one of the presents our cousins had just given her. (Unless it was chocolate or perfume; she always kept those.) She would say something like: "Here, Anne gave me this, but I don't want it. Take it." I've noted in recent years that my mother has a similar habit, and I've taken to buying her things that I also like, as she will undoubtedly give it back to me in the days or weeks that follow.

Although my mother reminds me of my grandmother in many ways—her appearance, her fierce independence, her compassion, and her meticulously clean house—she is not the same type of mother my grandmother was.

When one looks at one's own family, it's natural to look for common traits. Who shares the same eyes? The same smiles? The same mannerisms? The same quick temper? When I look at my mother, I see no similarities between the two of us. She's fair and I'm a brunette. I love wine, nice restaurants, cats, dogs, and good books. She's a teetotaler who enjoys crafts and puzzles and is definitely not an animal lover. She's also a fabulous cook, where I can barely boil an egg. Still, we are very close. We talk in person or on the phone most days. When my daughter was born—which was around the time my parents' divorce was finalized—she moved to the city to be closer to us. She never had that same connection with her mother.

Their relationship was always a bit strained. Grammie wasn't an easy person to live with, given her mood swings and straightforward manner. They talked often and were always good to each other, but there was sometimes tension. Luckily, I'd never seen the difficult side of Grammie that my mother had. My grandmother was a complicated woman, but I never doubted she loved us, and we loved her unconditionally.

As children, we don't often question why the adults around us are the way they are. They were already like this before we came into this world, and that's just the way it is. But as I've learned through asking questions about my Murray ancestors, there is sometimes a story or explanation.

Grammie loved her stories—and I loved to listen to them. It should come as no surprise that the tale of the quintuplets was her favourite to tell. But she also often spoke—almost whimsically so—about her young life. About how beautiful she was and how she spent her days on the local beaches getting a golden tan. About the handsome men she met, and the long car rides they'd take her on. Her good old days. She also spoke about life on the farm. "One time out on the farm" were words she spoke often.

Because the family farmstead was gone long before my time, I always assumed my grandmother grew up there. I imagined a carefree childhood of playing in the fields, picking apples from the orchard, and riding horses. But early into my Murray family research, I came to the realization that wasn't the case at all. In actuality, Grammie only lived on the Murray farm as a young adult, and the circumstances that led to her living in Little Egypt were unique. What I learned about her life there reaffirmed my belief that her story deserved to be told. She faced more hardships than most, and they formed the person she would later become—strong, solitary, and loving, just in her own way.

At some point, all we become is memories, whether we live three days, twenty years, or one hundred years. Annie Margaret (Murray) (Brooks) Brown lived eighty-nine years.

My grandmother would most certainly not have been pleased had I written about her life while she was alive, but now that she is gone, I think she might even like being immortalized in a story.

LITTLE EGYPT, 1930S: THE LITTLE GUEST HOUSE

There were three places the teenagers liked to hang out in New Glasgow in the winter of 1935—the movie theatre, the hockey rink, and the Goodman Department Store, commonly referred to as Goodman's. Conveniently, all were located in the bustling downtown.

Saturday nights were particularly busy. All the stores were open, and cars lined both sides of the streets. People came and went every which way. Men blared their car horns at cyclists. Mothers dragged their crying children. Couples walked hand in hand.

Annie Murray and her girlfriends had spent an early evening shopping at Goodman's. The girls weren't particularly tired, but they had run out of things to look at in the shops and it was time for them to catch the bus back home to Trenton.

The late winter air was cool, so they stood near the store's entrance to catch the bursts of warm air that escaped when shoppers opened the front door. The light above the shop door shone down on them as they chatted, laughed, and waited. The bus arrived irregularly, and they hoped they wouldn't be there long.

A group of young men cut through the parking lot with hockey bags over their shoulders and sticks in their hands. They were headed for the nearby rink.

One of the men took notice of Annie. It might have been because she was illuminated by the overhead light, or maybe she smiled at him to get his attention. (Both Annie and the young hockey player were known in their respective towns for their winning smiles.) Regardless of the reason, he stopped and walked up to her.

He introduced himself as Sterling Brooks.

She introduced herself as Annie Margaret Murray. She often used her middle name, as she liked the sound of it.

Sterling wore his dark brown hair cut short in the back and long in the front, a style many of the young men wore those days. A piece fell in his eyes, and he flipped it back. She thought him handsome.

Annie was used to being noticed. She was tall—but not too tall—with beautiful features and long wavy blond hair that made her friends envious. She had already had a few boyfriends, although none of them serious.

The pair talked casually for a few minutes.

Sterling told her he played for the New Glasgow 7Up hockey team, which was part of the Pictou County Junior League. This meant little to her, as she wasn't much of a hockey fan. She would later learn that he was something of a local star. He was from New Glasgow. She was from Trenton. The two towns were neighbouring, but as he was a few years older—he was twenty-two to her eighteen—it wasn't surprising they hadn't met.

Sterling Brooks in his New Glasgow 7Up hockey gear.

He asked her to go see a movie sometime.

She said yes.

The movie they watched might have been *Home on the Range* or *The Bride of Frankenstein* or *The Little Colonel* with Shirley Temple. Hollywood movies were popular in 1935, even in small-town Nova Scotia.

Annie and Sterling spent that spring and summer getting to know each other. He called on her at her house on Monroe Street in Trenton, or they met in town. They would go to a movie or just for a stroll to check out the shops.

When they were out together, people often stopped and stared. The pair could have been Hollywood celebrities. She was lovely, and he was handsome and charismatic. They were a couple with a bright future ahead of them.

When Sterling wasn't playing hockey, he worked as a brickmaker in New Glasgow. It was a job he had done for many years part-time with his father. The job would turn into a full-time gig when spring came around and the rinks closed up for the season. Although the pay wasn't great, it was something he could pick up seasonally to keep the money coming in when he wasn't on the ice.

Annie and Sterling were married that September at St. George's Rectory, a Church of England parish. Sterling's mother would have liked them to be married in her Catholic church, but as Annie's family was Protestant, that wasn't an option. There was some tension about the marriage on the Brooks's side. Annie wasn't the Catholic girl they wanted their son to marry, and they weren't going to let her forget it. The wedding ceremony was small and simple. The couple's good friends John and Marjorie Smith stood for them.

Newly married, Sterling and Annie needed a home to call their own. Unfortunately, their options were limited. Annie had never worked a day in her life, and although Sterling's salary was steady with the two jobs, it wasn't high.

On their behalf, Annie's father, Andrew, inquired about a little "guest house" that was sitting vacant out on the Murray farm.

Annie's Uncle Geordie—he'd been the youngest of John and Elizabeth's children in 1880 when the quints were born—lived and worked on her grandparents' farm, and had proposed marriage to a woman on a neighbouring farm a few years earlier. In anticipation of starting a family with his fiancée, Geordie built a small house behind the Murray farmhouse. Just before the wedding was to take place, the woman broke off the engagement and moved away. Geordie was a perpetually solemn-faced man—possibly because of being jilted—with a thick body and a square face. He liked his whisky and working the farm, and not much else.

The little house he built for his runaway bride had sat vacant for years, and Geordie agreed to rent it to Annie and her new husband at a low family rate.

In addition to Uncle Geordie, other Murray relatives called the main Murray farmhouse home. Another uncle, Thomas, lived there from time to time to help with the work, as did other members of John and Elizabeth's brood. It was a revolving door, of sorts. There was always a need for additional hands on the farm, and the old house was always there with a bed for someone to sleep in, and enough food to feed another relative. And because of Sarah's disability—which left her unable to look after herself—there always had to be a woman there to care for her. Over the years, her sisters took turns, but they eventually had families of their own and moved on. At one point, when Libby was away, Grammie's older sister Elizabeth moved out to the farm to look after Sarah and to cook and clean for the men. Elizabeth, named after her grandmother, was a kind and gentle woman and took on her new life without complaint, but it was at the expense of having a husband and family of her own.

Annie and Sterling's little "guest house," as they called it, was a simple place. It had two bedrooms upstairs and a small kitchen and sitting room on the main level. There was a water pump out front and a two-seat outhouse out back.

It wasn't much, but it was a home. And they had their entire lives ahead of them.

CHAPTER 4:

WOMEN, MIDWIVES, AND WITCHES

When I was pregnant with my daughter in 2003, I had only one thing written down on my birth plan. I wasn't concerned with playing soft music, taking videos, muted lighting, or even pain meds—all of which are typical birth plan items—I was only concerned about the use of forceps. I didn't want them.

In a forceps delivery, a doctor uses an instrument shaped like a pair of salad tongs to help guide a baby out of the birth canal. When my aunt Phyllis—my mother's older sister—was born in 1937, forceps caused brain damage during her birth.

Although I realized giving birth in 2003 was considerably different than in 1937, the risk was still there. I'd read about rare cases of skull fractures, nerve damage, cervical cord injury, swelling, and trauma to the baby's eyes and brain. Forceps are rarely used today and, according to the National Centre for Health Statistics, the number of babies delivered with forceps or vacuum extraction is only about 3 percent. I knew that in all likelihood I didn't need to worry. I did anyway.

My due date was Christmas Eve, which is also my husband's birthday, and although he doesn't love having his birthday over the holidays, we thought it was fitting that our first child might share that day with him. But the holidays that year came and went without a baby. I was enormous and uncomfortable and desperate to have the baby out. Finally, on New Year's Day, the doctor took pity on me and started the induction process. Although labour began as predicted, it didn't progress quickly. They gave me an epidural and Demerol for pain relief, but the Demerol made me violently ill. I started throwing up and didn't stop. Forty hours later, when the baby still wasn't born, I was too weak and tired to deliver. I remember seeing a moment of panic on my doctor's face when the baby became stuck. They immediately wheeled me into an operating room in case I needed an emergency C-section. Luckily, I didn't. Instead, they overlooked my one birth plan stipulation and used forceps. At that point, I didn't care. They had no choice. You can't foresee or plan for the events of childbirth. Anything can happen. For me, the dreaded forceps were the best choice. My baby daughter was born perfectly healthy; the only signs of distress were distinctive L-shaped purple bruises on each of her little round cheeks.

What I remember most about my daughter's birth—besides the pain and joy, of course—were the trained women at my side. My doctor, Dr. Jim, was an energetic woman who actually had two patients in labour at the same time and spent the early morning hours running between two rooms. The anesthesiologist who gave me the epidural was also a woman, as were the many nurses who stayed with me throughout the forty-plus hours of labour and during my recovery. They had all helped countless birthing women before me, and I had confidence in them.

Women have been helping other women in childbirth for as long as babies have been born. The word *midwife* stems from an old

English word that means "with woman." But for many centuries, that critical skill of midwifery had a rather dark cloud hanging over it. Childbirth was ruled by folklore and superstition. The Church considered some forms of midwifery—in particular, anything that made the woman more comfortable or the baby come more easily—as meddling with natural processes and thus a violation of God's will. For example, the use of forceps—or as they called them, birthing spoons—wasn't just illegal, but a mortal sin. From the fourteenth to the seventeenth centuries, midwives in Europe and beyond ran the risk of being accused of witchcraft.

One of the earliest historical recordings of the idea of witches occurs in the Bible, in the book of 1 Samuel. As the story goes, King Saul sought the Witch of Endor to summon a dead prophet to help defeat the Philistine army. The story is believed to have been written between 931 and 721 BC.

Over the centuries, it's estimated that millions of people—85 percent of them women—were accused of being "witches" and killed for it. Their punishment was not only horrific, but often very public. The accused might be stripped naked and have all their hair shaved off. They would be beaten and starved. Many were hanged, beheaded, or drowned and their bodies incinerated to protect against "post-mortem sorcery." Some faced the flames on the stake and endured an excruciating death.

A witch's crimes could be anything from blasphemy or religious heresy to politics or immorality. Women were accused of forming a coven if they were caught gathering together in any kind of organized group. Those with medical or obstetrics skills were of particular interest and often suspected of having some form of magical powers. There were some key characteristics that many, but not all, of the accused women had: they might be poor (or the opposite—financially independent), they could be middle-aged or old, they may have had sex out of wedlock, perhaps they complained in public, had few or no children, or they had a distinctive mole or birthmark. Essentially, any woman could be accused of being a witch.

Accusations were not limited to any one country. Trials were held in Belgium, Scotland, Bavaria, France, Switzerland, Sweden, Germany, the Netherlands, and many other countries, including America, with the infamous Salem witch trials in colonial Massachusetts in 1692 and 1693. But the witch hysteria really built momentum in Europe during the mid-1400s. There was even a guidebook for hunting witches in the fifteenth century. The *Malleus Maleficarum* (which translates as "Hammer of Witches") was a best-selling manual written by Heinrich Kramer, a Catholic clergyman, and published in 1486. It was a guide for identifying, hunting, and exterminating witches. It includes this damning assertion: "When a woman thinks alone, she thinks evil."

In addition to accusations of witchcraft against midwives, birthing women themselves had other issues to worry about. The sex of a child, for example, was often thought to be within the woman's control (although this was not universally believed). King Henry VIII of England famously blamed his wives for not producing male heirs. Similarly, women were often held responsible for any abnormalities or congenital defects in children. In fact, accusing women of a problem can go back to Old Testament times, as Eve was the one blamed (in some cultural and religious beliefs) for the original sin of eating the forbidden fruit.

One of the most famous witch trials in German history took place in 1587, against a German midwife named Walpurga Hausmannin. An old woman and recent widow, Walpurga had worked as a midwife for nineteen years before she was arrested and accused of sorcery. The exact reason for her arrest is unknown. Under extreme torture, she confessed to a number of bizarre crimes, including eating roasted babies and murdering children and drinking their blood, all while working as a midwife. In all likelihood, she told these stories to make the agony of her torture stop. Such torment would often result in false confessions. Regardless, the Church sentenced her to burn at the stake. In particular, it was her confession of having had sex with the devil that demonstrated a relationship between witches and the devil, and this idea was used in countless other witch trials throughout the ages.

When healers were accused of witchcraft, entire communities bore the brunt, as those healers were often the only person for miles around with any medical knowledge. And not only were the women persecuted for their skills, but they were also not permitted to train in the traditional medical field. University-trained physicians became the only recognized healers, and women were shut out until much later.

The book *Witches, Midwives & Nurses: A History of Women Healers* by Barbara Ehrenreich and Deirdre English offers an interesting look at women's struggles throughout the years. It details the male takeover of health care, from witch trials in medieval Europe to the rise of the medical profession in the United States. The first edition, which was published by the Feminist Press in 1973, begins with a rundown of all the roles women have played over the years: from healers and midwives to unlicensed doctors to teachers and pharmacists. "They were called 'wise women' by the people, witches or charlatans by the authorities. Medicine is part of our heritage as women, our history, our birthright," Ehrenreich and English write. According to the authors, their book was "written in a blaze of anger and indignation." Times have changed considerably since then, but the subjects covered in the book were still topical and relevant enough to warrant a second edition of the book in 2010.

Maria Murray's childbirth experience in 1880 was vastly different from mine in 2003. I was in a sterile environment, surrounded by experienced delivery doctors and nurses and the latest medical equipment, and Maria gave birth in a small, cold, isolated farmhouse in the middle of nowhere. She had only her neighbours, family, and a small-town doctor and pharmacist to help.

Without prenatal care, there was no way Maria could have anticipated her quintuplet birth, but she may have noticed some specific differences with this pregnancy. She might have experienced pregnancy symptoms earlier, such as more severe body changes, increased fatigue, nausea, and emotions. She was at a greater risk of pregnancy-associated conditions, such as hypertension, anemia, diabetes mellitus, eclampsia, and placenta abruption. It's also likely she went into labour earlier than with her other pregnancies, as most quintuplets are born around thirty-two weeks. But if she experienced any or all of this, she would not have known the reason.

At that time, sanitary precautions were not considered important and in a poor farm household like the Murrays', there would be no extra clean towels or blankets. Childbirth was agonizing and dangerous. Some statistics show a staggering mortality rate of one in eight mothers in the 1800s. If something went wrong, such as a breech birth or extended labour, the danger increased. If a woman started bleeding, there was little the midwife or doctor could do to stop it. Even births that were problem-free could develop complications, and infection could set in. Some women suffered from something called childbed fever, which started a few days after birth and led to poisoning or sepsis and eventually death.

In the few newspapers articles that exist about the quintuplets' birth, Maria is described as a strong and healthy woman. From all knowable accounts, she managed the birth and recovery without complications—and in fact went on to bear five more children in the years to come.

I have a picture in my mind of what Adam and Maria Murray's farmhouse—the birthplace of the Murray quints—might have looked like, which I formed from the small details I've gathered over the years. Constructed around 1870, Adam Murray's farmhouse was built about the same time as Grammie's maternal parents' home (the Allans) in nearby Point Forty-Four. Aunt Ginger noted the supposed similarity between the two houses. In her grandparents' home, bedrooms were located upstairs, with a small parlour beside the kitchen with a bed. When needed, this space was transformed into a birthing room, as it was conveniently located close to the wood stove in the kitchen, where women would boil the water and heat the blankets. It also likely served as a comfortable spot for cradling and rocking babies to keep them warm. Doris once showed me a newspaper clipping that was of an unrelated story but featured a photo of a giant old-style kitchen stove. "That's what the Murray quintuplets' kitchen looked like," she told me.

The Murray quintuplets may have been born in a parlour room such as this.

My grandmother and other Murray family members also remembered the detail of green curtains or blinds with gold tassels in Adam and Maria's home. These were used to wrap the newborn babies in when the family ran out of blankets. It's one of the few details I have of the house that helps to set this scene. It was also my grandmother's favourite detail— "They didn't have enough blankets and had to take the curtains off the windows," she used to say every time she told the story. This part was never recorded in the newspaper accounts or books and remains one of the few details that have travelled through the years solely by word of mouth, handed down through the generations.

I once watched an episode of *Grey's Anatomy* where a woman was expecting quintuplets. When the babies were delivered via a planned C-section, I counted at least thirty-five people in the delivery room. *Grey's Anatomy* is fictional, of course, but is also known to paint a fairly realistic picture of modern health care. They had a team for each baby and experts on hand in preparation for every possible scenario.

On that cold, wintery morning of February 15, 1880, there was no team of specialists ready with incubators and expert knowledge of premature infant care. In fact, people couldn't even imagine the possibility of five babies born at once. To be fair, it didn't happen often. The odds of naturally born quintuplets are about one in 60 million.

Because the Murray quintuplets were three girls and two boys, we know they were not all identical. They could have been fraternal, with five unique egg/sperm combinations, or a combination of fraternal and identical. Two or four of the babies could have been identical twins, with twin girls and/or twin boys in the mix. It's hard to say, as the doctor made no formal notes. We do know each baby's length and weight, which was recorded by the coroner. Each Murray quintuplet was around three pounds, a healthy weight for a multiple, as the average size of a quint is two pounds twelve ounces. There's a very good chance that if they had been born today, the Murray quintuplets would have survived.

Interestingly, that same year of 1880 saw the first warm chamber incubators introduced at a hospital in Paris by a doctor named Pierre Budin. The device—which was originally inspired by a zoo incubator used for raising chicks—had a removable cover, a place for the infant (the incubator), an air-inlet for circulating steam, a hot water tank, a spirit lamp (an alcohol burner with an open flame), and a thermosiphon (a method of passive heat exchange that is also commonly used in heat pumps and furnaces). It worked, and it was saving lives. The incubator solved the problem of thermoregulation, the natural internal process that allows a body to maintain its core internal temperature. Budin wanted to share his invention with the world, but no one in the medical profession would listen to him. It wasn't until Martin Couney, a German doctor who apprenticed under Budin, entered the scene that the idea was taken seriously.

Dr. Couney's interest in saving premature babies was a personal one. His own daughter was born prematurely and lived to adulthood, thanks to her father's care. Most people at that time assumed premature babies simply wouldn't survive—because they rarely did. Dr. Couney wanted to both improve the survival rate for preemies and educate the public about what was possible. He decided that if hospitals were not going to use the technology, he would. He used fairs and exhibitions to attract crowds and money for his neonatal care projects. Parents of preemies had nowhere else to turn and took their tiny babies to him. By having the infants on display, along with careful nursing practices, Dr. Couney proved before everyone's eyes that the incubators were a success, as the infants lived and thrived. He took his incubators all over the world, including Paris, Atlantic City, and New York, and most famously to Coney Island, where premature babies were a popular sideshow from 1903 to 1943. "All the World Loves a Baby" declared a sign above the entrance to the exhibit. And it was true. Hundreds of thousands of people paid to see them. His display not only saved thousands of children's lives, but it did more to educate the public on infant care than anything else had.

Couney's teachings went beyond the incubator to other methods of care. As noted in Dawn Raffel's *The Strange Case of Dr. Couney: How a Mysterious European Showman Saved Thousands of American Babies* (2019), although the incubator was standard in hospitals in postwar, baby-booming America, doctors were still using techniques that didn't work. Starving babies was one such technique that had mixed results. "One theory held that since two- and three-pound humans can easily die from vomiting and diarrhea, it would be wiser not to feed them at all for the first few days. It worked! No more unwanted effluvia! Unfortunately, the patients died of starvation," wrote Raffel. When hospitals began to follow proven methods for treating premature infants—such as using incubators—Couney considered his life's work a success and the Coney Island exhibit closed.

Ensuring the survival of a premature infant in the late nineteenth century posed significant challenges, even for educated professionals. It took special care and years of experience and training. And even then, the odds were not good.

As the Murray quintuplets were born half a century before the life-saving incubator was an option, the babies most likely died of a combination of factors. Because most multiples are born premature, they don't have those crucial last weeks in the womb to gain much-needed weight. Various vital organs, such as the lungs and brain, may not have fully developed. The babies might also have had trouble breathing and may have been incapable of maintaining a constant body temperature. Not to mention the problem of feedings. How would one woman breastfeed five babies? A wet nurse would have been necessary, but in a small rural community such as theirs, finding one would have been next to impossible.

According to Judith Young's *Nineteenth-Century Nurses and Midwives in Three Canadian Cities, 1861–1891*, The Register of Qualified Midwives, published annually in *Belcher's Farmer's Almanac*, began in Halifax in 1880. Between ten and fourteen midwives would be added each year. These midwives qualified for the registry with a diploma from a well-known midwifery centre or certification by the provincial medical board. Certification of midwives became compulsory in Halifax in 1872, although it was not strictly enforced. How could it be? In a rural area such as Little Egypt, a doctor was not just a quick phone call away. There were no telephones at the time, and the county didn't even have a hospital.

Even though a birthing mother did not have the luxury of a doctor's careful watch, sonograms, or heart monitors, she did have the support, stories, and knowledge passed down to her by the women in her life—her mother, sisters, aunts, grandmothers, cousins, friends, and neighbours.

In 1892, a diphtheria epidemic broke out in New Glasgow. As there was no hospital to confine the sick, doctors set up a temporary infirmary in a house. The same had happened almost forty years earlier, during a smallpox outbreak in 1855. It wasn't a sustainable situation. The area needed a more functional, permanent structure for the sick. According to *The Aberdeen Hospital New Glasgow, N.S.: A History, 1895–1988*, architects and builders were consulted, and a group of concerned residents formed a committee. They stirred up public interest by circulating brochures that noted 175 cases of contagious diseases in New Glasgow and Trenton that were worsened by "the impossibility of treating them properly in the houses where they occurred." Residents were certain a hospital would save lives.

The four towns of Westville, Pictou, New Glasgow, and Trenton came together to support the project. Estimates for the new twenty-two bed red brick facility included a construction cost of $8,800, plus $2,200 for furnishings. Food and medicine were estimated to cost 41¢ per day per patient, and staff salaries for the year were about $864. The actual total cost came to $14,968, which was a considerable sum for the times.

They broke ground on the project in 1895, and the hospital opened its doors to patients in 1897.

Located on the west side of New Glasgow, the Aberdeen Hospital was named after John Campbell Hamilton-Gordon, who held the title of Baronet of Nova Scotia, First Marquess of Aberdeen and Temair, Seventh Earl of Aberdeen, and Governor General of Canada from 1893 to 1898. His wife, Lady Aberdeen, had a great affection for Canada and had been instrumental in founding the Victorian Order of Nurses and the Local Councils of Women.

The 1897 *New York Hospital Review*, published by the Roosevelt and Bellevue Hospitals in New York, said this about the new facility: "The furniture is all white enamel, perhaps the only hospital in Canada except the Royal Victoria in Montréal where the entire outfit is of enamel work. The operating room is equipped with electric lights so that in the case of an accident work can be done by night as well as day."

In its initial newspaper story about the hospital, the *Eastern Chronicle* wrote: "Now that the hospital is really underway, an important factor in the furtherance of the work is the women, and forthwith an auxiliary was formed." Auxiliary members and volunteers dedicated hundreds of thousands of hours annually to raise funds for needed equipment, bursaries, and other important programs. They held community teas and suppers, pantry sales, and garden parties. They also sponsored musical performances and lectures, including a public lecture by Alexander Graham Bell in 1899.

Although the hospital expanded many times over the years, it eventually closed to make room for a much larger, superior facility on the east side of town. The population was booming after the Second World War, and the hospital needed more room for obstetrics and general nursing areas. The present-day Aberdeen, where I was born, opened in 1955. It currently has about 104 beds and serves approximately 48,000 residents.

The period of the early 1900s in women's history feels especially frustrating to me. While townsfolk may not have been burning witches, societal norms still restricted women from pursing certain professions, such as becoming doctors. Many women were eager to make a difference in any way they could. In addition to raising money through ladies' clubs and auxiliary organizations, some were activists for peace, social reform, and for their own human rights. However, these battles were generally fought by the educated and the wealthy. Middle-class women found their options even more limited—they could be nurses or teachers, or they could stay home. My female Murray ancestors, for example, would have been at home on the farm, raising children, preparing meals, and tending to domestic chores. Although significant changes were on the horizon, they remained largely out of reach for the average Nova Scotian woman.

Even after the witch trials of the fifteenth, sixteenth, and seventeenth centuries became a dreadful memory, conflicts between surgeons and midwives remained. Doctors believed modern medical techniques were safer for mothers and babies and pushed to control obstetrical care. Midwifery was banned or heavily regulated in parts of the United States and Canada in the nineteenth and twentieth centuries. This was a disservice to many, as North American doctors at the time were often far less competent than midwives.

Britain legislated midwifery in England and Wales in 1902. The US adopted a similar model in 1925, which was a combination of nurse and midwife. In Canada, midwifery is currently regulated under provincial jurisdiction. The first Canadian midwifery training program was offered in 1993, and there are now seven education programs offered in the country, each requiring four years of baccalaureate-level training. Gone are the days when generations of women pass down this knowledge in farmhouse front parlours.

Everything I know about midwifery I learned from watching the BBC series *Call the Midwife*, which chronicles the lives of nurse midwives living and working in London in the late 1950s and 1960s. The show—based on the real-life memoirs of midwife Jenny Worth—offers us a window into the profession of that time. (Note that midwifery practices in general varied from region to region and were influenced by factors such as culture and medical advancements.) On the show, the midwives and doctors work together. In the early seasons, the nurse midwives would travel to a woman's home to deliver the baby, and if anything started to go wrong, someone immediately called for the doctor. This is how I imagine the birth of the quintuplets unfolded. The female neighbours—my great-great-grandmother Elizabeth Murray and likely Flora Chisholm, another untrained midwife—were there to help, and when something started to go wrong (in this case the birth of more than one infant) the doctor was sent for.

The 1950s, '60s, and '70s were critical decades for women's health-care issues. By 1958, almost all childbirths had moved from the home to the hospital. Grammie, for example, gave birth to all of her children at the Aberdeen Hospital, yet she herself had been born at home. The oral contraceptive pill first became available in the early '60s, although only married women could get prescriptions before 1967. Delivery-room doors began opening for men in the '60s, but it wasn't until the 1970s that men stayed for the actual birth. Today, the image of the cigar-smoking celebrating father is a thing of the past, with dads expected to be at their partner's side for the birth of their child.

The popularity of *Call the Midwife* is often credited with instigating a resurgence in the demand for midwifery among pregnant people, as well as of other practices that see women helping women in childbirth. Women today want to take control of their own prenatal care, and involving a midwife is one way to do that.

I didn't have a midwife when I had my children, as my fear of the dreaded forceps—or something else going terribly wrong—led me to choose a hospital birth. Midwifery also wasn't mainstream in Nova Scotia in 2003 and 2004, but it has become considerably more popular in recent years. I know women who loved the experience of having a midwife or who are planning to use one in the future. It would almost seem the professions associated with childbirth have come full circle, with female attendants, nurse midwives, doulas, and women obstetricians at delivering women's sides once again.

LITTLE EGYPT, 1930S: A TRAGEDY

It was the first game of the provincial playdowns against Antigonish. Sterling, who played forward, was going for the puck when he collided with an opposing defenceman. It was a bad hit, and Sterling went down with a severe injury to his groin.

The trend for hockey gear at the time was short pants and long stockings. The short pants—or "hockey knickers"—provided some padding for the thigh and groin area, but not much. Given the level of fast play on the ice in this league, injuries were common. Sterling was confined to a bed in the Glace Bay hospital for a few days, but at age twenty-five and otherwise in perfect health, he was itching to get back out on the ice. He travelled with the team home to New Glasgow a few days later for the final game of the provincial championship series. He told everyone he was feeling pretty good and ready to play.

As it turned out, Sterling wasn't well enough to play and stayed at home on the farm the night the team played in New Glasgow. He was pale and Annie could see he was unwell. He was also irritable but insisted he was fine. His team, The Miners, then went on to play in Moncton, where they faced the Maroons for the Maritime title. Sterling went with them. They won, but Sterling began to feel ill immediately after the game. Something was seriously wrong. He was rushed back to New Glasgow, and by the time he reached the Aberdeen Hospital, he was in critical condition.

Annie left the girls with her parents and went directly to the hospital where she sat at her husband's side. He was in even worse shape than she had feared. When he was conscious, he screamed and cried in pain. An infection had set in and spread to other parts of his body. Doctors performed emergency surgery on his abdomen, and for three more days his condition remained poor.

Annie held his weak hand in hers. He was fighting for his life; she could see it in his eyes.

"If I manage to beat this," he said to her, "I promise to be a better husband to you."

With him away so much playing hockey, their three short years of marriage had been hard. His words were exactly what she wanted to hear. She told him, with wary confidence, that he would be better soon.

The next day he showed a slight improvement, and everyone was hopeful he was on the mend. But the following day his condition worsened once again. This time, the doctors insisted he needed a blood transfusion if he was going to pull through.

Blood transfusions at that time were becoming more common but remained dangerous. One of Sterling's former teammates, his friend Grant MacGillivray from Antigonish, volunteered to give his blood. The transfusion took place on Friday afternoon.

But it didn't help. Sterling declined even more rapidly.

Sterling was sharing his hospital room with another patient, an old man dying of cancer. The room stank of death and decay. "I'll never forget that smell," Annie said later. "It seemed to be wafting equally from both beds. It was just awful."

Sterling continued his fight through the weekend, but on Monday morning, he died. He was just two months shy of his twenty-sixth birthday.

CHAPTER 5:

THE TOWN, THE TIMES

In order to truly imagine the birth of the Murray quints, and the role my great-great-grandmother had played in delivering them, I needed to know more about life in the 1880s—life in general, and in Nova Scotia specifically. What did Nova Scotia look like in that era? How did day-to-day life unfold? What were the common jobs? What entertained people? How advanced was technology? With these and other queries in mind, I decided to visit the province's Museum of Industry, hoping to shed some light on that period.

I hadn't been to the museum in many years. One morning, when I mentioned to my father that I was headed there to do some research, he told me I needed to talk to a friend he referred to as "Appleseed."

"Why?" I asked. I had heard Dad mention this man before, but I had never met him.

"He works at the museum and knows everything there is to know about the place," Dad told me.

“Is he working at the museum today?” I asked.

“Well, no,” he said. “He’s laid off for the season, but that doesn’t matter.” My father insisted on calling him and arranged for me to meet Appleseed at the museum entrance at two o’clock that afternoon.

There’s a reason the Province of Nova Scotia built its Museum of Industry in Pictou County. The area has a long, rich history in manufacturing, natural resources, and trade—from coal mining, forestry, fishing, and agriculture to the manufacturing of paper, cars, tires, glassware, soda pop, and clothing. But the county’s past isn’t all prosperity and riches. Local author James M. Cameron once wrote, “Pictou County’s story is littered with the wreckage of defunct industries.” It’s this past—the good and the bad—that defines the individual towns. And the museum, like all museums, exists to remind us.

When my children were young and we visited New Glasgow in the summers, we’d go to the museum on rainy days so the kids could run around. The building has plenty of open space for them to explore and enough interesting historic displays to keep the adults captivated. Although the topic of obsolete industry might sound a little dull, the museum isn’t. With more than thirty thousand objects in its collection, the massive building houses actual trains and a real printing press, as well as the province’s first motor car within its walls. (Interestingly, the car is called The McKay; sadly, I could find no family connection.)

The museum’s physical location is also historical, situated near two of the oldest industrial sites in the province: The Foord Pit, which was once the deepest coal mine in the world, and the Albion Railway, the first passenger and freight railway in the country. Even the museum parking lot contains a landmark of local history: the giant stone ruins of an old pumphouse that was used to dewater mines flooded with water from the East River during an 1880 explosion.

As I was driving there, it occurred to me that I had no idea what Appleseed looked like or even what his real name was.

My father owns a service station called The V, aptly named for its location at a distinctive V in the road. Although the original building—built by my great-grandfather McKay in 1928—has been replaced numerous times over the years, the general location has always remained the same. Today, it isn't so busy with customers as it is with my father's friends, most of them retired, who stop by to hang out. Beside the station is an old apartment building that my father also owns. My grandfather built it in the 1950s. The apartments are small and out of date by about sixty years, but Dad is friendly with all the tenants and has nicknames for many of them. Appleseed is one such person.

I needn't have worried about finding him. It was September and tourist season was over, so ours were the only two cars parked in the lot that afternoon.

I walked over to meet him, introduced myself, and promptly thanked him for meeting me.

He extended his hand. "Steve Cook," he said.

Steve is a lanky man in his mid-fifties with a casual, laid-back look about him. We walked up to the front desk together, where he attempted to explain what I was working on to the ticket counter guy. Steve referred to the Murray babies first as twins and then quadruplets. I corrected him. Neither Steve, who had worked at the museum for sixteen years doing demonstrations and interpretations, nor the guy at the desk, had ever heard of them. I told them most people in the county hadn't.

I didn't expect to find any direct information on the quintuplets there. I was more interested in what the town was like in 1880. Still, my new helpers were keen to find something. They discovered the museum had a clip of the Dionne quintuplets singing on the radio as part of a temporary exhibit, but it had recently been disassembled, so I couldn't listen to it. One of them also remembered that the Murray quintuplets were the answer to a trivia question in a board game about Pictou County. I had heard about this game but had never played or even seen it.

"Do you have a copy of the game?" I asked, thinking I might actually find something concrete that day.

"Yes," said the man at the desk, "but it's also in storage and there's no way to access it."

My heart sank. Everything was just out of my reach.

He then searched a database and found reference to the Murray quintuplets in a book called *Along the Shores of Little Harbour*, which I hadn't heard of before. He searched the local library online and told me there was a copy there that I could check out.

I took my time walking through the museum. I read all the information plaques, and I asked Steve questions about each display. We stopped for a while at a miniature town landscape.

"This is an example of what a Pictou County town looked like back then," he told me, pointing to tiny, simple homes and horse-drawn carriages. "Each community had its own shops, churches, schools, mills, and sometimes industries."

As we walked through the museum, I experienced a journey back in time. I witnessed how the province had evolved over the last two hundred years—from farmers, fishers, and craftspeople to communities and towns shaped by industry. I saw how they once spun wool and made quilts, and I watched a demonstration of how the first grist mills worked. There were displays on the town's first beauty salons and electric streetlights, as well as its first trains, cars and machine shops.

Up some stairs and off the beaten path from the rest of the displays we found the museum's coal-mining exhibit. Pictou County is home to one of the worst modern coal mine disasters in Canada. In 1992, a methane explosion at the Westray Mine caused the deaths of twenty-six miners. The mine had only been open about a year and it never reopened after the tragedy. Everyone from the area remembers where they were when they heard about it. I was in grade 11 then, on a school trip to Halifax for a drama competition. Our teacher told us the news. She spoke cautiously, in case one of us knew someone who worked at the mine, which luckily wasn't the case. Still, it had happened in our community, and we were all anxious to hear about the rescue. In the days after the explosion, crews desperately searched the rubble for survivors. The county, the country, and the world stayed glued to their television sets waiting for news.

Looking at the mine photos made me think of a personal connection I had to the disaster. About a week after the explosion, my father came home from an afternoon crushing cars at his scrapyard and said he wanted us to see something. He took me, my brother, and my mother back out to the scrapyard property, which is about a ten-minute drive from his gas station in New Glasgow. We walked to a spot of dusty earth in the middle of the yard, and he scraped the ground with a stick. When he did, thin lines of pale grey smoke rose up from the ground. He did it again and the same thing happened.

"What is it?" we asked.

"I have no idea," he said.

We stood and watched the strange, mystery smoke for some time.

The next day, my father called the Department of Natural Resources and explained what he saw. They told him that given the location of his land, it was probably smoke coming up from the still-burning Westray mine. The mine followed a seam of coal all the way from the town of Westville in the very direction of Dad's scrapyard. The entrance to the mine was almost ten kilometres away. It was surreal to think we were standing right there, on a beautiful, seemingly normal spring day, with the mine deep below us. Years later, a permanent memorial was built for the miners not far from my father's land; officials determined the memorial site was around the spot where many of the men had been trapped and died.

Westray was far from the first mining disaster the county experienced. From 1827 to 1945, Nova Scotia was Canada's leading coal producer. People came to the province to work, and they stayed. They raised families and built their lives there. But prosperity came at a high price. Pictou County mining was particularly dangerous because of the thick seams of methane-producing coal in the ground. Every mine in Stellarton between 1827 and 1880 ended with fires and explosions. A disaster at the Drummond mine in Westville in 1873 killed sixty men and boys. The Foord Pit explosion in Stellarton in 1880 killed fifty. Those are just some of the devastating tragedies that forever changed the families who lived there.

Although I never knew of any Murray family members who worked in the mines, there were some on my grandfather McKay's side. The odds are good that there were other miners in distant branches of my family tree. It was a rare Pictou County family that didn't send members underground over the centuries.

The museum's mine exhibit includes a searchable "fatalities database," which is also on the province's website, containing more than 2,500 names of people who died in fatal accidents in Nova Scotia's mines and quarries between 1838 and 1992. Many of these deceased were listed in the museum display. There were numerous Murrays among them.

In 1880, the world was changing. The first electric streetcar was installed in Indiana. The journal *Science* was first published in the United States (with financial backing from Thomas Edison). The Black Donnelly massacre grabbed headlines in Middlesex, Ontario. Competing circus owners P. T. Barnum and James A. Bailey joined forces to create the Barnum & Bailey Circus.

Medical breakthroughs were also on the way, but many people—especially babies and children—were still dying from diphtheria and other incurable illnesses. A look at newspapers of the time shows a barrage of ads offering cures and preventions. A large ad in the 1880 *Eastern Chronicle* for Scott & Bowne Manufacturing Chemists promised "Consumption can be cured. Is a fact attested by the highest medical authority in the world." It went on to say that the trick is "the persistent use of Scott's Emulsion of Cod Liver Oil with Hypophosphites of Lime and Soda." The ad then lists complimentary quotes by American physicians. Another ad stated, "Prevention Better than a Cure" as its sales spiel. "To protect you from tuberculosis, wear Hygeian Underwear, Wet-Proof Boots, Broadway Clothing, Royalty Hats, Cravenette Raincoats, Umbrellas. Sold by Sutherland & Co., Main St. Westville, N.S."

In 1880, Pictou County was growing rapidly, with a population of more than 32,000—the county today is home to fewer than 44,000 people—and was a booming industrial centre for coal mining and shipbuilding. In a few years the county would have its own hospital and post office and multiple hotels, but in the 1880s it was still establishing itself as a collection of small towns. The last to incorporate was Trenton, which was the closest in proximity to the Murray settlement. The year 1880 was not only significant because of the quintuplets' birth, but also because it was the beginning of development and community growth for the area.

Trenton was quite literally forged around the industry of making steel. In the 1870s, only sixteen people lived in what was then known as North New Glasgow or Smelt Brook. In 1878, that all changed when Hope Iron Works outgrew its small plant and relocated to the shores of the East River in what would soon be named the town of Trenton. The iron works was later called the Nova Scotia Forge Company, and the company made ship fastenings and other forged products, including railway car axels and ship anchors. In 1883, it produced the first steel in Canada. In 1912, the Eastern Car Company began manufacturing railway cars next door to the steel mill. It was believed to be the largest facility of its kind in Canada at that time.

The work was dirty, involving long hours and tough manual labour, but it was employment, and the industry drew workers from all over to the area. Houses were built, small businesses were established, and a town began to surface from what had been nothing but trees and a dirt road years before.

A shipyard was added to the mill years later. During the Second World War, a portion of the facility was used by the government to make ammunition. At its peak, the company employed 2,800 people and grew to a floor space of 742,709 square feet. The collection of factory buildings forms a long and industrial-looking structure, with small windows, a high roof, and numerous smokestacks, which in its day pumped constant black smoke into the air.

In the 1990s, the plant's future became uncertain, and in 2007, what was then called Trenton Works closed its doors. The plant reopened for a few years to build wind turbines, but the reprieve was short-lived and the facility closed again, this time permanently, in 2016.

Many of the people who worked there did so for their entire lives. It was all they knew. They spent their money locally and the town thrived. My great-grandfather Andrew Murray, Annie's father, was one of these men. But the facility had other connections for me as well. My grandmother Annie met my grandfather Fred, her second husband, when he was in town to clean the dangerously high windows at the plant one summer. And my paternal grandfather, Alex McKay, worked there throughout the entire Second World War when the plant manufactured ammunition, which allowed him to avoid the draft.

The town also had a long history with glassworks, including The Nova Scotia Glass Company, Lamont Glass Works, and Humphreys. Many of the plants' glass dishes are on display at the museum and can still be found in Nova Scotian homes. They are considered collectibles today. Some people likely have no idea there's a Nova Scotia-made Ribbon and Star goblet, a Crown fruit bowl, or a Tassel and Crest butter dish lurking in the back of their cupboards. Aunt Ginger showed me several pieces she owns, as well as an old collector's book showing all the patterns.

The town grew from a booming hub of hard-working, blue-collar families to a town that has, in some ways, lost its identity. Today, the streets are generally quiet and few businesses and restaurants remain in operation. As a community, it still celebrates its industrial heritage, however, like many towns with a similar background, Trenton has had to shift its economy and continues to evolve.

All this local history was captivating, and I was learning more at each exhibit we stopped at, but one of the things I was looking for at the Museum of Industry was information on the telegraph service. I wanted to know how the story of the Murray quintuplets reached the world. Although the telephone was invented in 1876, Pictou County had yet to have a single telephone in 1880 and relied on its telegraph and telegram service for communication. But what did that look like? How did it work? And where was it located?

I inquired about the telegraph service at the museum front desk on my way out, as I was surprised I hadn't seen anything about it. The man at the desk said it wasn't part of any permanent displays.

Steve and I parted ways, and I drove over to see my father at The V. I knew he had a few old books on Pictou County, and I wanted to check them out.

My father is a collector of old things. He has enough old gas pumps, cans, and service station signs to open a museum of his own. He also has a rather extensive collection of books. I asked him if he had any books that might help with my research.

"I don't have much," he said from behind the counter at the station. "But I can take you up to the loft to take a look."

Located between his garage and the apartment building, he has a personal apartment set up on pillars that acts as a segue between the two structures. People call it "the loft" or "the bird's nest." He built it after he and my mother divorced in 1998. He never actually lived there; it's more a place for him to store his collectibles. He also eats his lunch there on weekdays.

The place was dusty but cheerful, with lots of natural light from the big front windows and lush, green plants everywhere. I took a

Along the Shore of Little Harbour—with a handwritten inscription inside the jacket that read: "To: Annie M. Brown"—which the author discovered among her father's book collection.

quick glance at his bookshelf and then glared at him. "You have every single book ever written about Pictou County here," I said, and I would know, seeing as I'd been tracking down old historical volumes all over the place for months.

"You think? I haven't actually looked through them in years."

Dad never takes time to read books, and I've stopped buying them for him as Christmas gifts. For him, books are another thing to collect. He says he'll read them on a rainy day, but when the rainy days come, the books remain untouched.

The first book I pulled off the shelf was *Pictou Parade* by Roland H. Sherwood, which I knew had a short story about the quintuplets in it, as I had recently borrowed a copy from someone else.

"This is a signed copy," I said when I opened it.

"Yeah, a lot of them are signed. People pick them up at auctions and estate sales for me."

The next book I picked up was *Along the Shores of Little Harbour*, which was the book the front desk guy at the museum had told me about, the book I was going to check out at the library. It was a small book that had, in all likelihood, been lovingly compiled by a group of history-loving neighbours. I flipped it open and found a handwritten inscription inside the book jacket. "To: Annie M. Brown, From: Ginger and Fraser MacLean, Sunday, July 15th, 1984."

"Did you know this was my grandmother's book?" I asked him. "Was this Mom's?" As my parents had long been divorced, it seemed odd for him to have a book that had belonged to my mother's mother.

"No. Someone picked it up at a book sale for me." Like so much of his stuff, he had no idea where it came from. But it was possible it came from a sale of my grandmother's donated things after she passed away. If that was true, it was a sign that stories are not only passed down through the generations, but also around communities. In this case, it came full circle!

I left the loft with a box of about twenty books. I took everything that seemed interesting. Most contained nothing about the quintuplets, but they did have old stories of the county, and I thought they might tell me something of value.

On the way to my car, Dad asked me if I wanted to see an old scrapbook he had found that belonged to his mother, my grandmother Alice McKay. I followed him into one of his old apartments. I had been in this particular unit once before. An old man Dad called Mahoney—I have no idea of his real name—used to live there. I had dropped something off to him years before and remembered the derelict state of the place. The man had been a cat lover, a smoker, a serious hoarder, and a terrible housekeeper—a problematic combination in a one-room apartment. He was a friendly man who mumbled when he talked and smiled often. No one had lived there since Mahoney died years earlier. I wondered momentarily what happened to his cat.

Dad had converted the apartment into a neat little storage area for his overflowing collection of antiques. Everything of Mahoney's was gone. The smell of cat pee and cigarettes was also gone, replaced with the scent of old, mouldy boxes.

The scrapbook he was talking about was open on top of one of his antique cabinets and he started flipping through the pages, which were yellowed from decades spent in some other storage space. There were clippings of me and my brother and our unexceptional sports accomplishments, and page upon page of obituaries. There was also a story about my grandmother McKay's full recovery from breast cancer back in the 1980s. The cancer had returned years later, and she lost her second battle. Even though it was twenty-five years ago, I felt the loss anew when confronted with the story. I imagined her carefully cutting out her clippings and gluing them onto the pages of her scrapbook—a book that had sat forgotten for decades after she was gone.

I love that my father keeps things like this. Not many people do these days. If only someone on the Murray side of the family had kept a scrapbook or a diary, I would have something concrete from the time. All we have is what previous societies leave us. In the Murray family's case, it's a handful of mostly forgotten stories and a few sparse newspaper articles, none with even a single quote or comment from the family.

I noticed a picture hanging on the wall by the apartment door. It stood out because it was the only thing on any of the walls. It was a coloured sketch of a very tiny building, almost as small as an outhouse, high on the riverbank overlooking the East River and old New Glasgow.

I pointed to it. "What's this?"

"That's the old telegraph building."

I explained how I had just been looking for information on the town's telegraph service at the museum. I now at least knew what the old building looked like. My research had come to me in a roundabout way that day.

I had one more question for Dad before I left. "Why do you call Steve 'Appleseed'?"

"He came over to the garage one morning after watching some story on television about Johnny Appleseed. I never knew who he was and had to ask him. Now I just call him that. Everybody does."

LITTLE EGYPT, 1939: PHYLLIS

Annie didn't know what was happening when her three-year-old daughter, Phyllis, fell to the ground and began shaking violently.

She gathered all three girls—Ginger was two and Doris four—and ran to the big Murray farmhouse, and one of her uncles drove them into Trenton in the farm's horse and buggy. From Trenton, they all took the bus to the hospital.

The only explanation the doctors could give Annie was that Phyllis's brain may have been damaged during her complicated delivery with forceps, and that damage was causing seizures. There was little that could be done. Antiepileptic drugs did not exist in 1939.

It was a hard reality for Annie to comprehend. Her daughter looked perfectly normal, with her round cheeks, big blue eyes, and blond ringlets. Plus, she was as smart as could be.

The seizures didn't let up. They became more and more frequent. When Phyllis would have one of her "episodes," Annie would have to drop what she was doing and run to her daughter to hold her head and keep her from injuring herself. Other times, something would just come over Phyllis and she would start running, seemingly for no reason. Annie would have to run after her before she crashed into something or fell down.

The child couldn't be alone for even a second.

Annie tried her best, but she couldn't handle the three girls on her own. Annie's parents took Doris to live with them in Trenton.

Doris loved living in town with her grandparents, where she had a little room of her own. She would shuffle between their home on Monroe Street and the homes of her three maternal aunts—Nina, Christine (Teenie), and Doris—who lived nearby. Everyone had recently started calling Annie's sister Doris "Big Doe," as there was now a little Doris in the family (whom they aptly nicknamed "Little Doe"). As she grew older, Doris liked that she could run outside and find other kids and cousins to play with. It wasn't like being out there on the Murray farm, isolated and lonely. She visited the farm frequently with her grandfather, and she stayed on the odd occasion, but she would never live on the farm again.

When Ginger turned five it was time for her to go to school. She walked the three miles into Trenton all alone and attended the small schoolhouse with other kids her age. Phyllis was a year older and didn't understand why she couldn't go as well. But there were no separate classes for kids with disabilities nor teachers who could give her special care. Plus, her "episodes" would have scared the other children. Children like Phyllis didn't get to go to school. That didn't stop the little girl from wanting to learn. She could say her ABCs backwards before Ginger could even say them forward. When Ginger left in the mornings, Phyllis cried.

At home, the two girls did everything together and were very close. It often fell to Ginger to look after Phyllis. She knew just how to hold her sister's head and use a pillow to help soften the violence of the convulsions. When a seizure was over, Phyllis was left disoriented and confused, and Ginger explained where she was and what was going on. The girls also shared a bed, and Phyllis sometimes had seizures through the night.

In the summers, Annie's Aunt May's daughters would come to the farm and home-school Phyllis. They were quite ladylike and had to be waited on while there. One was a teacher and the other a secretary. They taught Phyllis to read and to print. Although the little girl worked hard and was genuinely curious, the seizures caused brain damage and learning challenges. Her skills never went beyond the ability to write words in childlike block letters.

CHAPTER 6:
LOST STORIES

My first attempt at telling the story of the Murray quintuplets was in 2008. I was working at the *Halifax Daily News* at the time and had pitched it as a feature story to the Sunday editor. She loved the idea. It was a little-known Nova Scotia tale that she felt would be of interest to readers. The article was scheduled to run on February 17, which was near the time of the 128th anniversary of the babies' birth on February 15.

I was *finally* doing something with this quintuplet story that I'd been thinking about since I was a kid.

My research began with my grandmother, even though she had died in the summer of 2005. I had all her newspaper clippings in a folder, and I spent an afternoon poring over them. I wrote down little details she'd told me over the years. I walked myself through that trip we took to the Murray farm back when I was nine. Still, I was left with more questions than answers. I desperately wished I had asked her more when she was alive. And why hadn't I written things down? Gotten more details? They say tomorrow isn't always promised, and this was a time when that truth hit me. I always knew I wanted to write a book about the Murray quintuplets, yet

I expected when the time came, my grandmother would be there to help.

My grandmother's sister Teenie was still living at the time. She was the last of the seven lovely Murray sisters and my favourite of all the great-aunts. Teenie was one year older than my grandmother and would be turning ninety-three at the end of February that year. She still lived in her longtime home in Trenton. I thought I would pay her a visit and see what she could tell me. My mother came along for the visit.

I had been to Teenie's house many times over the years. It was a white two-storey four-square–style home facing Trenton Road, just a stone's throw from the turnoff to Little Egypt. It was also only about a block from where she grew up. There had once been a little convenience store in the basement of her home. It was long ago, even before my mother's time. I love the idea of old stores—old stock, old prices, and old-time storekeepers—and tried to picture what that might have looked like.

My mother and I went to the back door and let ourselves in. The house was the same as it had been my entire life. Just inside the doorway was a neat line of shoes and winter boots, and a colourful Easter basket full of stones. The basket had been there since I was a kid. I never asked where it came from. Probably something one of the grandchildren set there for just a moment and never retrieved, and then it just stayed there, no longer noticed. Part of the scenery.

We walked into Teenie's neat, clean kitchen. The room was bright, white, and spacious, with a galley cooking area in the corner. Although always welcoming, it wasn't a place we went for meals or family gatherings when I was growing up. Get-togethers were usually at our home, with my mother as host. We typically just stopped at Teenie's house for short visits. My mother says she was an amazing cook, but I don't remember eating much there. I would have a glass of ice-cold water from the orange pitcher in her fridge or a chocolate from a box.

Teenie was expecting us. I had phoned the day before to arrange the visit. Years ago, we would have just dropped in, but her hearing wasn't good, and we didn't want to surprise her. Hers was typically a quiet house. When I had visited in the past, it was usually just her at home. Her husband, Rod, spent a lot of time at their cottage over the years and had passed away in 2002. We heard the TV blaring from the living room and followed the sound, knowing exactly where we'd find her.

Teenie was in her big firm armchair facing the television. Her daily set-up was much the same as my grandmother's had always been. It's not uncommon for some older people to sit comfortably day-to-day in the same chair, in the same spot. I remember my grandparents on my father's side had their own matching his-and-hers chairs facing their television. When I asked my mother about her own grandmother, Grandma Murray, she said she always remembered her sitting in the same spot across from the wood stove, knitting or crocheting.

In contrast to the bright kitchen, Teenie's living room was dark. A covered front porch blocked much of the natural light to the room. She was wearing a light-coloured cotton housedress like my grandmother used to wear, and glasses attached to a chain around her neck. Her hair was whiter than I remembered it, and her skin was a shade paler. She looked so much like my grandmother, it was eerie.

When Teenie saw us, she slowly stood up.

"Oh, Lori Anne and Twila," she said. My great-aunts always called me Lori Anne. Although I never corrected them, it didn't feel like my name. I was just Lori now. "Come in, come in. Sit down."

She smiled and her kind eyes crinkled the way they always did. That was one of the biggest differences between her and her sister—Teenie's eyes were kind, whereas my grandmother's were always a bit sad.

I hadn't been there in a long time. Too long. Life was busy and I'm terrible at visiting without my mother to instigate. We sat on the long sofa beside her chair. I asked about her grandchildren and great-grandchildren, who all live away, but our conversation was riddled with her saying, "What was that?" and "Sorry, I didn't hear you." I told her about my kids, but I don't think she heard a word. She nodded and smiled anyway.

Without my asking, she jumped into the reason for the visit.

"I can't tell you anything about those quintuplets," she said.

"You must remember something," I insisted, the journalist in me suspecting she knew more than she believed she did. People often do.

My great-aunt paused a moment to think. The problem wasn't her memory—her mind was still as clear and sharp as ever. I could tell. She talked about visiting the farm on occasion as a child and a few details about the family, but as for quintuplet stories, she just knew the basics—her grandmother delivered them, they used the blinds as blankets, and they were buried in the basement of the house.

"It was Annie who knew the stories," she said. "The rest of us didn't spend much time out on the farm. Our lives were in town. But Annie, she lived out there in Little Egypt."

When Teenie and the rest of the Murray siblings were young adults, the towns of Trenton and New Glasgow were booming with new industry jobs, people, and activity. To them, she told me, the farm in Little Egypt seemed a world away.

Teenie suggested I visit her cousin Jean Schaffer. "Jean spent a lot of time on the farm when she was young."

My mother knew her, but it was the first time I'd ever heard the name "Jean." The mention of this mysterious cousin intrigued me. Did Jean hold the key to the family secrets I desperately wanted to unravel? The mere thought of meeting her gave me hope. I couldn't wait to hear her stories and untold histories. I was also thrilled at the prospect of encountering yet another Murray relative.

Jean's house in New Glasgow was on a little side street that I'd driven by thousands of times over the years. We knocked on the door and it was answered immediately by a tiny, elderly woman with dishevelled blond-grey hair. I suspected she might have been hovering behind the door, waiting for us. Jean gave us a distracted smile. I could tell she wasn't the type of woman who spent her days watching TV from an armchair. Her step was quick and her energy high as she ushered us in.

The house was old and plain with brown hardwood floors and beige walls. It lacked any sense of modern decor or colour, yet it was full of interesting things. There were antiques and collectibles everywhere I looked. There was a steep staircase opposite the entryway door, and my first reaction was curiosity. I would have given anything for a few minutes to snoop around.

We sat in her living room. Her old-style sofas and chairs were set in the centre of the room and arranged in a little oval. Behind the front room was a dining room. The antique table and sideboards were covered in stacks upon stacks of old newspapers. I'd never seen so many newspapers piled in one place, and I worked at a newspaper.

Jean and her sister Pearl had lived in the house together until Pearl's death a few years before. The two unmarried sisters had looked after one another most of their lives. Pearl had been unwell for her last years, and Jean had been her caregiver.

Jean offered to make tea and disappeared through the dining room into what I assumed was the kitchen, returning minutes later with a proper serving tray and pot and three china cups.

As luck would have it, Jean did know the story of the Murray babies. It was mostly the same story I remembered from my grandmother, but I loved hearing it again. She told me about her time on the farm and how she and Pearl spent their summer vacations there every year. She told us that part of what they did on these vacations was home-school Phyllis. They were the cousins who had taught Phyllis to read! She also told me about a woman named Mona who lived in Adam and Maria Murray's old house. She described her as a silly but pleasant woman.

"She always wore rubber boots, even when the weather didn't call for it," Jean remembered. "She'd come over to the farm to borrow things and stay for a visit. She'd stand around the kitchen chatting with Aunt Libby and eat a slice or two of pie before she'd be on her way."

"Was she a Murray?" I asked.

To this Jean shrugged her tiny, thin shoulders. "I'm not sure. I assumed she was a relative."

"Did she live there alone?" This Mona interested me. She sounded like a real character, much like Jean herself.

"I think people stayed with her sometimes. They could have been relatives, but I'm not sure. If I remember correctly, they weren't the best sort of people. They would raid our gardens in the summer and steal from the farm."

Jean could not recall when Mona died or what happened to the old house, which she described as small and shabby. All she really remembered was the big wood stove. "It was the focal point of the home," she said.

This reminded me that it's the feeling of a place that people often remember, not the little details. When she visited, she clearly remembered the sense of unity the wood stove offered. I imagined this Mona standing by the stove in her rubber boots, cooking or warming her hands on a cold winter day. It would have been the exact same wood stove that kept Adam and Maria's family warm and fed for decades, and the quintuplets warm during their short lives.

Although this day of research gave me little in the way of new information, I relished the time spent with my mother and visiting family. My mother never had a problem with picking up the phone and asking someone if she could just stop by. I'm terrible at making time for extended family, and I don't take my kids to visit relatives nearly as much as I should. Because of this, they will never know most of their second cousins. I suspect it's a generational thing. Today, it's easier to text someone or simply keep up to date on what they're doing through social media. For example, I don't need to see my relatives in person to know how much my cousins' kids have grown: I see their hockey achievements, their first days of school, and their vacation photos on Instagram and Facebook. I, like many, have become lazy when it comes to visiting in the traditional sense—despite my deep interest in my family's history. There's sometimes a whisper in the back of my mind urging me to reach out more, to organize get-togethers, to make more of an effort. Then I think, "I'll do it later." But, as I've learned, sometimes later is too late.

I saw my great-aunt Teenie only one other time before she died in 2011 at ninety-six. I remember she was lying in a hospital bed, a white sheet pulled up around her neck. She was small and thin, having wasted away since our last visit. When she moved her arm to take my hand, I saw her wrinkled skin covered in purple and black bruises from the back of her hand up her arm.

"Old veins don't work so well with needles," she said casually. "I'm quite a sight, aren't I?" Then she laughed, seeming completely aware of her situation. She was dying and was at peace with it. Her daughter had called my mother a few days before to tell her Teenie's condition. I left the hospital that day knowing I would never see her again. She died soon after.

Jean Schaffer died in 2012. It's hard to say if either of these women could have offered additional help for my story in the present, but I still wish they were around to ask. They had unique memories of the old farm and the old way of life. All of the members of my grandmother's generation have now passed away.

The next generation is also getting older. During my research for this book, my Aunt Phyllis—one of my mother's older sisters—passed away at age eighty-one. She had been unwell and unable to leave her bed, and the seizures she'd experienced as a child—the convulsions that had started on the Murray farm all those years ago—had beome more frequent. Although most of the Murray descendants in my family, especially the women, have been blessed with health and longevity, they will not be around forever—and unless their stories are handed down, those stories will die with them.

A few years before I started the research for my newspaper article, a Nova Scotia historian named Clyde Macdonald published a book called *Notable Events in Pictou County* (2005). Clyde, who is also a well-known Pictou County judge, had published numerous regional history books over the years. This latest instalment was short non-fiction stories on such forgotten topics as the time the circus came to New Glasgow in 1890, Sir John A. Macdonald's visit to Trenton in 1888, and the big New Glasgow fire of 1874. It also included a story on the Murray quintuplets. I thought Clyde, having recently researched the topic, would be a good person to talk to.

I'd met Judge Macdonald before, as his son and my husband are friends. I called him and he was happy to meet up and chat. He had done some research on Dr. William Fraser, the physician who'd (reportedly) delivered the babies, and he gave me what he had, including an original image of the doctor, which I scanned and then returned. He also showed me some historical maps of how the old Murray property in Little Egypt had been divided up amongst the brothers and cousins. Most of these details were already in his book. He suggested I talk to the family contact he had spoken with, Ernie Murray.

I called Ernie, who I guessed to be in his sixties at the time, and explained what I was working on. He was great to talk to, but unfortunately, he knew very little about the quintuplets. The family story hadn't been passed down as freely as I had hoped. Ernie is a direct descendant of Adam and Maria; his great-great grandfather Alexander Chisholm Murray was born two years after the quintuplets in 1882. Ernie's father, Leslie Charles Murray, was born in 1907, just a year before Adam died in 1908, and the family moved out of the farmhouse soon after. Ernie's grandfather had no memories of the farm to tell his son or grandson.

Near the end of our phone conversation, I asked Ernie if he knew where the quintuplets were buried. He became quiet for a moment and eventually said, in a guarded, even defensive tone, "It's a family secret." He would say no more on the subject. I tried to convince him that I had no intention of including that information in the story and that I wanted to know because of my personal connection to the family, but I had no luck. Our conversation ended soon after.

Ernie's response left me even more curious. The babies in question had been dead for 128 years. In all likelihood, they would not have been embalmed and would have decomposed quickly along with the rosewood casket (or caskets) they were buried in, a gift from a neighbour, as noted in a local newspaper story at the time. There certainly would have been very little left of their bodies in 2008. And although there had been a lot of public interest in the location of the grave more than a hundred years earlier, by now surely no one was looking for it except me. Still, his instinct, when asked, was protective. It was a secret kept so close that no one today actually knows it for sure, including Ernie.

He eventually told me the story he knew, but I would have to wait more than ten years for him to be ready to talk.

With everything I had discovered and not discovered, I wanted to go out and look at the Murray property myself. The beautiful rolling fields that were once home to my relatives and later owned by my Aunt Ginger—the same property I visited with my grandmother as a child—had been sold and new houses were built on the land. The property, as I remembered it, was forever changed. It had lost its magic, in my mind.

I asked my husband's uncle (by marriage), Bruce Ervin, if he'd come along with me. The property where Adam and Maria's house may have stood belongs to Bruce's brother and I wanted him to help me get permission to explore it. I had always wanted to search for the location of the old house again. This was my reason to do it. I felt fairly certain I remembered the spot my grandmother had showed me all those years ago.

We drove up to Bruce's brother's house early on a cold weekend morning. There were two homes at the end of the driveway, both hidden from the road by thick, dark forest. It was a grey day, and a few feet of snow blanketed the ground. Bruce's brother knew why we were there, but I wanted to check with the residents of the other house before I started walking around their land.

I knocked on the door and a woman answered in her housecoat. I explained who I was, my family connection to the property, and what I was doing there. She said she didn't mind us taking a look around. Their house was still relatively new, and she told me that during construction she worried they might turn up old bodies with their digging.

"I'd heard the stories about the old farm and was warned people may have been buried around here. No bodies were found, just big stones from the old farm fences," she told us with a laugh, pointing behind the house.

The big stones were visible in her yard, even with the snow, and could be seen scattered throughout the surrounding woods. I recognized them for what they were. The building method is called dry stone walling, which means a stone structure is built without filling or mortar to hold the stones together. Such primitive constructions are common in Nova Scotia. There's a walking path near our home in Dartmouth, NS, that has remnants of an old stone fence along it. Our property was once farmland before the area was developed in the 1960s; there's still a centuries-old farmhouse tucked away behind some newer homes across the street from us. There is also a similar-style rock wall near our cottage in Black Point, as it was once farmland as well. We have simply built new ways of life on top of the old.

As Bruce and I headed into the woods, I searched desperately for any kind of sign that may have indicated an old home foundation. I assumed that because my family's Murray farmhouse had a stone foundation, the other Murray house would as well. We walked through the woods until we reached one of the new homes on what was previously my family's property. I could see the house through the trees. It was enormous—beautiful and modern—and sat right around the spot my grandmother and I stood when I was nine.

Bruce and I spent a good portion of the morning walking through those woods but found no sign of the old homestead. There was one indentation—a large bowl-shaped hole in the ground—but it was so full of snow I couldn't tell what it was, and decided it was most likely nothing. I needed to come back at another time. Preferably in the spring, as fall brought too many leaves and summer meant ticks and overgrown greenery. My visit to the property offered nothing definitive for my story except a sense of place. I now had a good idea of what it might have been like there in February of 1880.

I have since looked at satellite images and found at least two paths that could have once been the road to Adam and Maria's property, which was later known as Mona's Lane. I also have some new clues—Doris had told me about the russet apple tree outside the house, and Ginger said there was a little pond nearby. They might still be there, although I knew it was unlikely. Still, I thought I might have better luck when the snow melted.

After gathering as much research as I could for my article, I typed up all my notes and began piecing together my story. On the Monday before it was set to run on Sunday, the story was still in rough form. I've been known to procrastinate on writing assignments until the deadline, but had cleared that day of all other assignments. I hoped to get a first draft completed before I left the office that evening. The Friday before had been a complete writeoff for me. Someone had organized a ski trip as part of an event the paper had sponsored, and I had gone. It was a long, fun day and we spent much of that Monday morning chatting about it in the lunchroom. But by mid-morning I was sitting quietly at my desk, head down, immersed in my work. I was surprised when the publisher of the paper tapped me on the shoulder. He and a man he introduced as someone who worked for the paper's parent company, Transcontinental, asked me and a co-worker to come with them. My immediate thought was that we were being laid off, which was surprising because the division of the paper I was working in, the weekly community newspapers, had been doing very well. In fact, I had heard the weeklies were making more money in advertising than the *Daily News* itself.

Nervously, we followed them down to a storage room on the first floor. There were a few other co-workers there, including people who worked in sales and design. It felt strange, us standing there secretly hidden away from the rest of the staff. Then the announcement came: they were closing the newspaper as of that day. They had gathered us together to let us know they were keeping the weeklies but shutting down the rest of the paper. We still had our jobs, but our friends and co-workers did not.

I was in shock. I had worked at the newspaper for ten years—my entire professional career at that point. It was just luck that had put me in the weeklies department at that particular time. On February 11, 2008, the paper that had been founded in 1974 and was one of only two dailies in the city, ceased to exist. Ninety-two people were given severance packages, and a handful were offered jobs at a new free daily that was being launched. It was devastating for everyone, even those of us who still had jobs. A newspaper is a unique place to work. A group of people with a vast array of skills—from writing and editing to sales and marketing—put together an important record of current events every single day. I couldn't believe it was over.

In the last twenty or so years, cities and towns all over North America have lost their daily newspapers, leaving many communities with no local news source whatsoever. It's disheartening when I think about how important old newspaper articles are to the research of historical events. Without old newspaper coverage there would be no record of the Murray quintuplets at all.

The closing of the *Daily News* also meant my article now had no home. I couldn't run it in my weekly community paper, as it had no connection to any of the neighbourhoods it served. With so much on my mind at the time, I simply shelved the story.

LITTLE EGYPT, 1880: NEWS TRAVELLED FAST AND FAR

The little Murray house had only one cradle, so later in the day on Sunday, February 15, 1880, the hours-old infants were swaddled in clean blankets—gifts from the neighbours—and lying in shoeboxes on the oven door (a detail that was passed down through generations in the Murray family and relayed to me by a relative).

The wonder of five tiny babies born at one time was something of interest to everyone near and far but, in particular, within the family. Someone may have taken a horse and sleigh to Maria's parents' home on Roy Island, a few miles northeast toward the ocean, to pick up her mother. It is understandable that Maria would want her family with her. Her mother, Jeanette Rankin—and possibly one or two of her seventeen siblings—might have travelled to the little farmhouse in Little Egypt. Jeanette herself was still in good health, and all eighteen of her children were living, which was an achievement for those times.

Maria was a strong, healthy woman. The newspaper articles did not mention a woman who was sickly. In all likelihood she would have had a long recovery—carrying and delivering five babies would have put a great strain on her body—but it can be assumed she was awake and speaking with family and guests.

By nightfall, the little Murray farmhouse was a busy place. The doctor and James Jackson eventually went home, exhausted. The babies were sleeping and there was little more they could do but wait and see what the night brought. Dr. Fraser might have promised to ask around and see what he could do to help the family's unexpected situation, including sourcing breast milk and finding donations of money and provisions. He assured them he would be back the next day. He no doubt warned them of the risks associated with babies born that small. There was limited knowledge of how to help preemie babies at that time.

Maria, in her vulnerable state, might not have fully grasped the doctor's warnings. But no mother would give up hope that her children would survive.

Newspapers near and far covered the story of the Murray quintuplets' birth. Five babies born at one time was unheard of. It made international news. For example, on February 17, 1880, the *Detroit Free Press* printed an article about their birth:

> *Nova Scotia: A LARGELY ATTENDED SURPRISE PARTY. Halifax, February 16—The wife of Adam Murray, living near New Glasgow, yesterday gave birth to five children, three girls and two boys, finely developed. All are doing well."*

On February 19, 1880, the *Arizona Daily Star* reported:

> *Mrs. Murray Does it Up 'Brown'— News Notes. At Halifax, Nova Scotia, yesterday, Mrs. Murray gave birth to three girls and two boys, all of whom are doing well. This is the biggest full-hand on record.*

("Does it up brown" was an expression that meant to do something well.)

Similar accounts ran in most large city newspapers all over North America. (None of them noted Maria by her first name—always referring to her as Adam's wife or Mrs. Murray.) Some of the babies, of course, had already died by the time these articles appeared. Follow-ups were never printed.

Between visits from neighbours and family, Maria and Adam decided on names. They named the boys William Fraser and James Jackson, after the doctor and the pharmacist. They named two of the girls Elizabeth MacGregor and Margaret McQueen, after prominent women in the town. (These were also the first names of the two daughters they had lost five years earlier to diphtheria. And Elizabeth was, of course, also the name of the woman who helped deliver them.) The first baby born, the little girl who was a bit smaller than the others, was named Jeanette Rankin after Maria's mother. The couple may have felt these were strong names that could bring their children luck. Three years before, they named a son "George" after the little George they'd lost to diphtheria in 1875, and he was a strong, healthy boy.

The family checked on the babies often, holding each of them in turn. Perhaps Maria tried to feed them. It's unlikely they showed much interest in the breast; premature babies typically need extra coaxing, as their capacity to suck and swallow is poor.

At some point that evening, someone touched one of the baby's round little cheeks and realized the child wasn't responding. The baby's eyelashes were still. Their little mouth was open but unmoving. Their chest was flat. Someone may have felt for breath but found none. There was nothing anyone could do. The family was heartbroken.

Then a second baby died that same evening.

And a third.

No one in the Murray family likely slept throughout the night on February 15, 1880. Maria was forever checking on her two surviving infants. The three deceased babies were wrapped in blankets and kept near the cold of the door. It didn't seem right to put them in the basement or the barn.

Maria had experienced deep sorrow when she'd lost the first George, aged six years three months, Margaret, aged three years seven months, and Elizabeth, nine months ten days old. The family may not have been expecting five new family members that day, but Maria would have felt each of their deaths as an unbearable loss. The line between living and dying is a fine one. Like a slim, breakable thread.

LITTLE EGYPT, LATE 1940S: THE SHOOTING ON THE FARM

Although Annie's little guest house was near the much bigger Murray family farmhouse, it was still a good five-to-ten-minute walk away, and despite its proximity across the field, the two were not easily visible to one another. There were no bright streetlights lining the nearby road. There wasn't even a light beside Annie's front door, as the house didn't have power. When night fell on the farm, everything was dark. Most of the family was tucked into bed for the night by seven or eight o'clock, when the sun went down.

Annie kept a bedtime schedule for the girls that was as routine as she could make it. One fall evening when Ginger was seven and Phyllis was eight, the family was out of their normal routine. Ginger had just gotten home from the hospital after having her tonsils out. Annie tucked the girls in for the night, but she stayed up for a while to finish a few chores by the light of her kerosene lamp.

Sometime later she was surprised to hear someone rapping on her front door. She knew it wasn't anyone from the farm, as they were all long asleep.

Nervous, she went to the door and yelled, "Who is it?"

A man hollered back, "Open the door."

She peered out through the front window to find two men on her front step. She recognized their faces. They were from Little Harbour. She also saw their car, which was parked sideways on her front lawn. She guessed they were on their way home from the pub in Trenton. They staggered about with a confidence they didn't deserve.

There was a rarely used shortcut people called "The Crossroads" between town and the Harbour Road that passed directly in front of Annie's house. Everyone knew a young widow lived there, and Annie was certain the two men were there with ill intentions. The men, she thought, probably had no idea there were young children in the house as well. Or maybe they were the kind of men who didn't care.

Annie yelled at them to get away from her door.

"You come in here and I'll shoot you," Annie said. It wasn't just a threat to frighten them off; she really did have a gun, and it was always ready and loaded.

At this point the men were trying to tear the door down.

The girls were crying in their room upstairs.

Annie went to the closet and got out the shotgun. She stuck it in one of the three holes along the bottom of the storm window. She aimed for the trees, and then she fired.

A strange, eerie silence followed. She didn't move for a full minute. Then, with her back against the wall, she let out her breath. She thought they must have left.

The next thing she knew, her house was being riddled with bullets. The men had gone back to their car and gotten a gun of their own.

Annie rushed upstairs to check on the girls. Up until the bullets started firing, they had been looking out the window and were in the direct line of fire. They were terrified but otherwise unhurt. She took their hands and rushed them down to the basement, where all three huddled together and listened for the car to drive away.

When she knew the men were gone, Annie opened the hatch door that led from the basement to the backyard. With the girls in their bare feet and nightdresses, the little family crossed the dark field to Uncle Jim's. Although Aunt Libby, Uncle Geordie, and Aunt Sarah all lived in the house at the time, Uncle Jim, the eldest son, had come home from out west earlier that year, which made the house his house.

Annie knocked on the kitchen door and got Jim out of bed. Somehow, the shots had not woken him. He let them in, and they slept there in the farmhouse parlour for the night.

The next morning, Jim started up his old Model T Ford and took Annie and the girls to the police station to report what had happened. The men needed to be punished, Jim said. Annie imagined many years of jailtime for them both.

But the police officers didn't take the situation as seriously as she'd hoped. After she told her story, the officers asked Ginger to tell them what she heard and saw. When they sat her down, the first thing they asked was, "Where would you go if you told a lie?"

The little girl didn't know what to say. What kind of question was that? she wondered. "I don't know," she said, and then continued with her account of the events.

The police came out to the little house to examine the scene; the bullet holes in the exterior walls could not be disputed, yet the case never went to court. Nothing ever happened to the two men. The police said that even though they were trying to break into her house, Annie had fired the first shot. She didn't have money for a lawyer, so the case went nowhere.

Annie said later that it was a very good thing the men didn't make it through the door that night, because if they had, she would have shot them dead.

LITTLE EGYPT, 1940S: THE SECRET BABY

Money was tight. Annie and the girls were living on a widow's allowance, which wasn't much. And during the war years they also had to deal with strict rations. Annie needed extra money to pay for music lessons for the girls—Doris played violin and Ginger played piano—so she took on part-time jobs. She worked at the Trenton gun shop during the war, making shells. She worked in a men's clothing store selling shoes. She cleaned someone's house for a year. And her uncles sometimes gave her money for doing cleaning at the farm and taking in their laundry.

Cleaning clothes wasn't an easy chore in the 1930s and '40s, as it involved fetching water from an outdoor well, boiling it, and scrubbing on a washboard. But cleaning was one of the things Annie enjoyed doing. She was proud when she could take a filthy sheet and make it white again.

Annie was also lonely. A widow at just twenty-three, she still turned heads when she walked through town. Although she was too busy with the girls to be out looking for a boyfriend, she would have liked a new husband and father for her girls. On occasion she would go out to a movie with friends or to a dance at the local fire hall. It was at just such a dance that she met a handsome RCMP officer who was stationed in the town for a time.

The man was charming and interested in getting to know Annie. She didn't know it at the time, but he was also married. When Annie became pregnant, her relationship with the handsome constable was over.

Husband or no husband, Annie would have kept the baby if she had been able, but her father made the decision for her. He told her the baby would have to be put up for adoption. Annie simply could not afford to feed another child. Her parents made the arrangements. They knew the family the baby was going to and were confident it would be a good home.

The pregnancy was kept as quiet as possible, but people still talked. When the baby was born at the Aberdeen Hospital, the child, another girl, was immediately handed off to the new family. As part of the adoption process, Annie signed away all her rights. She took an oath to never tell anyone she was the child's biological mother, or to have any contact whatsoever.

Unlike her three blond daughters with Sterling, this baby had dark hair like the father. But Annie didn't know this at the time, as she never laid eyes on the child. It would be many decades later, when this secret daughter was an adult and sought her out, that they would finally meet.

After Annie recovered from the birth, she went home to her little guest house on the Murray farm with Phyllis and Ginger. The baby was not discussed again.

Adoption is not an easy topic for many people. Stories like my grandmother's have, in the past, been shrouded in secrecy and shame—and the stigma has deep historical, cultural, and societal roots. An unplanned pregnancy clashed with both religious beliefs and the idea of a traditional family structure. Parents with an unwed daughter who planned to give her baby up for adoption might have employed various strategies, such as arranging a false marriage or "widowhood," citing illness or recovery, or sending her away under the guise of studying abroad or visiting a relative—all aimed at maintaining privacy and avoiding embarrassment. In my grandmother's case, she stayed hidden away on the Murray farm, safe from the public's eye.

Over time, general attitudes towards adoption have evolved, thanks to increased education, advocacy efforts, and changes in adoption practices. However, remnants of the historical stigma still linger. It is yet another untold part of women's history.

CHAPTER 7: THE TWO JIMMY MURRAYS

In my grandmother's stories about the Murray farm, she often talked about two relatives, both with the name Jimmy Murray. As in many families, names run through them, repeating in generations and branches like blue eyes or curly hair. One was her Uncle Jim, her grandfather's brother and the last man to run the farm; the other was a cousin she called "Raccoon Jimmy," whose father was a sibling to the quintuplets. Annie had few friends and relatives she was close with, and even fewer that she liked, but she always spoke fondly of both men. It was obvious that she liked and respected them. To me, they always felt like "characters" of the story, both having a connection to the land, the time, and the quintuplets.

Throughout my many hours of sifting through old newspaper articles, I came across a story about Raccoon Jimmy. (I'm not sure if other people called him that or if it was just her way of distinguishing him from her uncle with the same name.) The article

Murray still fishing at 85

By Ruth Sangster
Of Our Staff

BLACK POINT — James Murray, Black Point, will be celebrating his 85th birthday August 5. He will observe his birthday by celebrating he is still a healthy, lobster fisherman. Helping him celebrate will be his cat, Kit Kat, neighbors Charles and Elizabeth Jackson, and his step-daughter, Valerie Gregg.

Jim has been fishing for 63 years, mostly lobsters, but has also fished salmon and herring. In 1919, his first year of fishing he hauled 50 lobster traps. With the help of John Wilson, Little Harbor, this season they have hauled 150 traps. The lobster stocks are better now than they ever were, he says. He can remember a time when the fish plant had to close because there were no lobsters for the May 24th weekend.

In his younger days, he and Ken Cameron, Chance Harbor, went salmon fishing in Doctor's Brook, Antigonish. One day, while out fishing, they caught 28 salmon, all over 20 pounds. The prize catch was not picked up as usual so they had to take it to Pictou where it would be sold. It is a 50-mile trip to Pictou taking most of the day to travel. While in Pictou, a rain and wind storm started. After selling the fish, Jim decided to go back to dock the boat at Doctor's Brook. Cameron wanted to stay so he grabbed his rum bottle and ran.

Murray set out for the Brook despite the weather, following the coastline a mile from shore. While passing Big Island, darkness was setting in. Combined with the strong wind and rain, he could barely make out the coastline. Finally, after many long miles, Jim saw the old lighthouse at Arisaig, signalling an end to this stormy journey. Late that night, he landed the boat and hauled it out of the water.

Four days later, fishermen were still unable to fish because of the same storm. Friends could not believe Jim had made the trip and got back in one piece. For many years the streets of Pictou buzzed with the story of Jim battling the worst storm of the season.

Jim has missed only one year of fishing, 1983, when he broke his leg. He spent three months in hospital and the rest of the year recuperating. Apart from his broken leg, Murray has had a very healthy life. He rarely suffers from even a cold. He attributes his good health to minding his own business and hard work.

Jim Murray has worked at many jobs throughout his life and has never had a holiday. Jim has worked as a carpenter, a blacksmith, a millwright at Hawker Siddeley, has drilled wells, and sailed the ferry that used to run from Pictou Landing to Pictou. The ferry carried everything from cattle to people.

Jim is very aware of his ancestry. This year marks the 105th anniversary of the birth of quintuplets born to his grandparents. The five were born on February 15, 1880, however, none survived past the 13th day. One of his Quebec ancestors won the battle for General James Wolfe against the French on the Plains of Abraham. After Wolfe was killed in the battle, his ancestor led the troops to victory.

His family is known for living a long life. One of Jim's uncles lived until he was 91. Jim expects to live past the age of 100. He has certainly lived the first 85 years to their fullest.

Jim Murray and his companion, Kit Kat love being outdoors. Jim has been lobster fishing for 63 years, missing only one season. This season, he set 150 traps with the help of John Wilson, Chance Harbor. Jim will be celebrating his 85th birthday August 5.
(News Photo by Ruth Sangster)

An undated newspaper article about James MacGregor Murray, otherwise known as "Raccoon Jimmy," which notes the birth of the quintuplets to his grandparents 105 years earlier.

wasn't about his raccoons but about his many years of fishing, which he was celebrating that particular day as he turned eighty-five. At the time, he had been fishing for sixty-three years. He claimed he had missed only one year due to a broken leg. He told the reporter he'd had a long and healthy life, and rarely even suffered with as much as a cold. There's a picture of him posing with a large pile of lobster traps and his cat, Kit Kat. He's wearing dark work pants with suspenders, a thin white button-down shirt, a slouch hat, and a frown. The article ends by noting the birth of the quintuplets, born to his grandparents 105 years earlier. It was clearly his family "claim to fame."

James "Jimmy" MacGregor Murray was born in 1900 on Sinclair Island, only a fifteen-minute car ride from the Little Egypt farm. He was the son of George Rankin Murray, who was two years old when his famous siblings came into this world. Jimmy lived most of his life in Black Point, within walking distance of my own cottage. His place was even closer to Aunt Doris's cottage. She actually bought her land from Jimmy, who told her it used to be pea fields. (I always wondered why people sometimes called that stretch of road Pea Field Hill.)

It was at his farmhouse in Black Point that I met him when I was about thirteen. My grandmother spontaneously suggested we pay him a visit. "Would you like to see some raccoons?" she asked. "I know a guy with a family of raccoons living right inside his house with him."

My answer to her query was an immediate yes.

Upon our arrival, Jimmy came out into the yard to meet us. He was wearing rubber boots and a scowl. He gruffly invited us in. Grammie pointed toward a covered porch area, and there they were. Five or six grey-and-black furry creatures, all huddled together sleeping in a pile.

"Don't go near them," she warned. "Raccoons are trash-eaters. They carry disease."

My grandmother wasn't an animal lover. Nor did she understand why anyone would want a pet of any kind.

I took only one step closer. They were adorable, as raccoons are, but they had abnormally long toenails and sharp little teeth. I could see their wildness.

Contrary to my grandmother's interpretation of the situation, the raccoons didn't actually live in Jimmy's house. Sometimes he'd leave the door open, and they'd come into the porch, where we saw them that day, but they mostly lived in a tree beside the house.

When we were leaving, Jimmy showed us his "raccoon tree" where there were more than twenty of them snoozing away in the afternoon sun. These raccoons were spoiled in the way a stray dog will stay if you keep feeding him. Once a week, Jimmy would go to a local bakery where they would give him their out-of-date bread. Neighbours would also drop off their old bread at his home. It was his thing.

Jimmy's house is still there, minus the raccoons. It looks nothing like it used to. It's been fixed up into a charming, historic farmhouse home.

Everyone who lived in the area knew Jimmy Murray. George MacKenzie, a relative of my husband's and our cottage neighbour, knew him well. George, who is in his eighties, is a serious history buff. He and I chatted often during the few summers I worked on this book. He knew all about the Murrays. He knew all about most of the families who grew up in the area.

George would sometimes stop by our cottage and drop off old newspaper articles and obituaries, or we would sit around the kitchen table in his 140-year-old farmhouse, and he'd show me old maps and tell me tales about the people who lived nearby. He even had some handwritten notes that he and Jimmy had penned many years before, chronicling Jimmy's family tree. It was through these notes that I learned of the three Murray children who had died of diphtheria in 1875. The names of the quintuplets were there, too.

With me, George had found someone who shared his interest in preserving the past. It's surprising how few people are curious about their own personal history. I suspect part of the problem is that many people today are so engrossed in technology and their busy everyday lives that it leaves little time to reflect on their great-great grandparents from a century ago. Perhaps all they need is one small, interesting fact to ignite this interest. In my case, that spark was the fascinating story of the quintuplets. For others, it might be a harrowing war narrative, the tale of a secret baby given up for adoption, or a journey across the Atlantic in dangerous conditions—experiences shared not only by my family, but by many in the nineteenth and early twentieth centuries.

I remember one particular sunny morning when George stopped by and we sat on my front deck with coffee. Our cottage—high on a hill in the middle of what was once his family's wheat field—looks over his farmhouse, with a beautiful view of the ocean beyond. Although the area is slowly becoming populated with new residences, I remember when it was only fields. Off in the distance, the Prince Edward Island ferry travels back and forth. Over the water, eagles fish and flocks of seagulls soar.

We somehow got onto the topic of Jimmy that morning.

"Jimmy was rough, in a way. But he'd do anything for you," said George. "He used to help put our water pump in every summer. He was a well-driller, he built boats, and he was a fisherman—he even got the prize at the Pictou Exhibition for being the longest-serving fisherman."

Jimmy helped build many of the cottages in Black Point back in the 1920s, including my husband's family cottage, which is near ours. George also told me about an old family cemetery in the woods beside Jimmy's farmhouse, where the previous owners buried their dead. Apparently, you could once see the rocks that acted as markers, but he wasn't sure if they were still there. He told me about meeting Jimmy's first wife, Marie, when he worked out west for a time. And he spoke about a child they had lost. There was a second wife as well—Marjorie—who passed away in 1964.

Jimmy died in 1998, just two years shy of a century.

Although he hadn't really done anything extraordinary in his life, I sensed he was remembered more than other family members of that era. I had met the man only once and remembered him clear as day. He was "a character," of sorts, and I don't mean just in my story. His house in Black Point will forever be known as Jimmy Murray's house. Oscar Wilde once wrote, "There is only one thing worse than being talked about, and that is not being talked about." When it comes to remembering past generations, I believe this to be true. Of course, different people value different qualities, and what one person finds memorable or interesting, another may not. Still, it's the quirkiness of some individuals that leaves a lasting impression.

Uncle Jim, a.k.a. James "Jim" Murray, was born in 1875. He was five when the quintuplets were born on the neighbouring farm. Of all my mother's long-departed relatives, he is the only one I remember her ever talking about. One of the reasons he always stayed in my mind was because she told me she saw his ghost on the day he died.

"I was eight and had just gotten home from the hospital after having my appendix out," my mother said. "At the same time, Jim was in a quiet room at the hospital, which was where they put people who were dying, but I didn't understand that at the time. I had been in the children's ward just down the hall. Children weren't allowed in the quiet room, but I would sneak down to peek in at him anyway. The day I got home, I was sitting at our kitchen table having lunch and I saw Uncle Jim walk by the door. He always wore a black hat that was very battered and faded. I called to Mom and said, 'Uncle Jim's here.' I went to the door, but no one was there. I can still see him when I think about it. We got a call soon after that to tell us Uncle Jim had died."

They call this a forerunner. A supernatural sign that warns us of an impending death. Such ghostly events typically involve bells ringing or a knock on the door, or a visit from an apparition, as was the case with my mother and Uncle Jim. Although I love the *idea* of anything ghostly, my mother does not. So when she told me she saw a ghost, I believed her.

In 1926, while living out on the farm, Jim bought himself a brand-new Model T Ford. It was his pride and joy; the talk of the town. Not long after his big purchase, he decided to move out west to prospect gold, copper, and other base metals that were in demand. He wasn't a young man; he was in his fifties, but he had no family of his own and felt a calling for adventure. He put his precious Model T into storage on the farm and left to make his fortune. During his years away, he lived in various Canadian provinces, as well as a few American states, and spent many years with the Hudson Bay Mining Company north of Winnipeg. He eventually returned home and settled down to live with his sisters on the family farm. Although he didn't strike gold while he was away, he supposedly came home with a trunk full of cash.

The first thing he did when he arrived home was take his old car out of storage, where it had sat for almost twenty years. With a little work, the car still ran, but the canvas roof had disintegrated, making it a permanent convertible. Ginger used to drive with him on occasion, when she needed to get into town, but she would always jump out and walk as they approached her destination—before anyone saw her in the loud, ancient vehicle.

My mother recalls the car more fondly. Whenever Uncle Jim went into town, she and her childhood friends would wait on the side of the road for his return, as he always tossed them chocolate bars. "To this day, whenever I see a Jersey Milk or a Crispy Crunch bar, I think of Uncle Jim," she said.

THE EVENING NEWS, NEW GLASGOW, NOVA SCOTIA

THIRTY YEARS OLD this year is the Model-T Ford driven by James Murray of Little Egypt. A veteran himself, Mr. Murray bought the old car brand new in 1926 and he's been driving it steadily since. Yep, he still does.

Old Model T Ain't What She Used To Be But Gets Owner There Just The Same

A 1956 newspaper article about the author's great-uncle James Murray driving his 1926 Model T after taking it out of storage.

A reporter from the New Glasgow *Evening News* happened to drive past Jim in his Model T one day in 1956 and wrote a little story about him and his car. Jim, eighty at the time, called it "the best car that company ever produced." There's a picture too, with Uncle Jim behind the wheel. He's even wearing the old, battered hat my mother said he always wore.

CHAPTER 8: MULTIPLE DIMENSIONS

There is a little-known tale about multiples called *The Origin of the Welfs*, which is often attributed to the Brothers Grimm (although it is not part of their official collection). In the story, a countess comments on a poor woman who had three children in one birth. She states in public, "It is impossible that this woman had three children from one husband without committing adultery." Then, a year later, this same countess gives birth to twelve identical baby boys. Scared she will herself be accused of adultery, she asks a servant to drown eleven of the babies and she keeps one to raise. On her way to the brook, the old servant meets the count. He inquires about what she is carrying in her basket. At first, the woman tells him she is carrying welfs (the German word for puppies), but she eventually tells him the truth. The count orders the boys given to a wealthy miller to raise. He asks the servant to tell his wife nothing about their arrangement and to tell her that her wish has been carried out. When the boys are six, the count has the eleven boys brought to the castle. Being identical, it is obvious to everyone that the boys have the same parents as the count and countess' son. The countess faints at the sight of them. Once brought back to consciousness, she begs for mercy. The count forgives her. As a reminder of the miraculous event, the count renames his progeny. Instead of the Counts of Altorf, his entire lineage became known as The Welfs.

Twins have always been seen as curiosities. In some cultures, twins were thought of as ominous portents, in others they were considered lucky. In Greek mythology, twins were said to be conceived when a woman slept with both a mortal and a god on the same day. Twins were sometimes considered two halves of the same whole, or as a representation of oneself—one a doppelganger to the other, or like a shadow. They are occasionally portrayed as good and evil, and there are countless tales of twins sharing a deep bond—if one gets bitten by a dog, the other feels the bite. Is there any truth to the stories? I couldn't say, as I don't have a twin.

But I do know that not every story has a magical or fairy-tale ending.

Although women have been giving birth to multiple babies at one time since the beginning of humankind, few of these rare and miraculous births were documented before the nineteenth century. There isn't even an official medical record that the Murray quintuplets ever existed.

But fifty-four years after the Murray quintuplets were born, another Canadian household welcomed a set of quints. These babies survived. And their story was indeed well recorded.

The Dionne quintuplets were born in the little country town of Corbeil, Ontario, on May 28, 1934, when twenty-four-year-old Elzire Dionne went into labour for the seventh time. Elzire and her husband, Oliva, had been married for nine years and had five children, with ages spanning from eleven months to seven years. A sixth child had been lost to illness years before. The family lived in a modest log home that had no running water or electricity. They farmed but had very little.

Elzire couldn't wait for the doctor to arrive. When the first baby came, the midwives thought it was the smallest newborn they had ever seen. In Pierre Berton's book *The Dionne Years: A Thirties Melodrama*, the baby was described as "a grotesque creature with the legs of an insect and a disproportionately large head, bright blue in color and scarcely human except, oddly, for the large eyes with the long lashes and an appreciable shock of hair."

When Dr. Allan Roy Dafoe finally reached the home, he was astonished to see there were two infants and a third on its way. He delivered this baby, and then a fourth and a fifth. They had to scrounge for more tattered woolen blankets. Each baby was given a provisional baptism, as they were not expected to survive.

News of the Dionne birth travelled rapidly to the media, but the doctor was quick to be cautious. Quintuplets had never survived beyond infancy before, and he didn't hold out much hope. Still, the entire world was interested and invested in the babies' fates from an early stage. People flocked to the house—neighbours, family, nurses, local children, reporters, and photographers.

Despite the outpouring of interest, Elzire and Oliva were worried. The babies were born at the height of the Depression; how could they afford to feed five more children? In addition to the fear of not having enough money, Berton reports that the couple were embarrassed. One of the first concerns Elzire expressed to her husband after she recovered from the birth was, "What will the neighbours think?" They considered the five babies a catastrophe. They worried people would laugh at them and compare their unusual birth to that of pigs or dogs: "a litter of babies."

Those fears were soon realized. Not long after the Dionne babies' birth, someone from the Chicago World's Fair visited their house, asking Oliva if his daughters could be put on display in the Century of Progress Exposition. Oliva asked Dr. Dafoe his opinion, and the doctor told him he should make what money he could, as he thought it was unlikely the girls would survive. Oliva signed a contract and received a large sum of money. Although several safety conditions were worked into the contract, when the agreement became public, people were outraged. The contract was eventually cancelled, but Oliva Dionne had gone from down-on-his-luck father of quints to exploitative mercenary in the eyes of the public.

Four months after the Dionne quintuplets were born, the Ontario government became involved in their care. The government found the parents unfit to deal with the high-profile children, and the girls became wards of the state. They were put in the care of Dr. Dafoe and two others. A new nine-room facility—the Dafoe Hospital and Nursery, with an observation area and outdoor playground—was built for the quintuplets and their nursing staff. They moved in at the end of that September, and soon after, the hospital became a major tourist attraction called Quintland.

In the nine years Quintland was open to the public, more than three million visitors watched the sisters through two-way mirrors. There was no charge for visitors of Quintland to view the children, and approximately six thousand visitors would pass through in a day. People came from all over, generating more than $50 million in tourism dollars for the province of Ontario. The quints were used to market consumer items such as Quaker Oats, Colgate, Palmolive Soap, and Karo Corn Syrup. Some of the money from these sponsorships was put into a trust for the girls.

Throughout much of the 1930s, Émilie, Annette, Marie, Cecile, and Yvonne were "the world's best-known babies." They were more popular than even Shirley Temple or the young princesses of the time, Elizabeth and Margaret. Little girls all over the world had quintuplet dolls in their toyboxes and Dionne calendars on their walls. It was a mania that people had never seen before.

In 1942, when the girls were nine years old, Oliva and Elzire won their legal battle, and the girls were returned to them. The government wanted to put some distance between itself and the family. They built the Dionnes a mansion for the whole family —they called it the "big house" (it is now an Ontario seniors' residence)—but the girls were unhappy there and the family was divided. The media storm of their early years slowed to what the newspapers deemed their "happy ever after." Yet, in the sisters' own book, *We Were Five*, published in 1965, they claimed the years they lived with their parents were the worst of their lives, and the years in the hospital/nursery their happiest.

When the quints turned eighteen, they left their family home and cut off almost all contact with their parents and siblings. But their adult years were not easy either. Marie and Émilie both decided to become nuns. Marie moved to a convent in Québec and Émilie to a convent near Montréal. Émilie had been having seizures since she was twelve and wasn't supposed to be left alone. In 1954, at the age of twenty, she suffocated and died alone in her bed from an epileptic seizure. Annette, Cecile, and Yvonne each married, but all of their marriages failed. Marie died of a blood clot in her brain in 1970. In 1998, the three remaining sisters received a $4-million settlement and an apology from the Ontario government. The sisters were struggling to make ends meet, and the money came at a crucial time.

My introduction to their story was a 1994 made-for-TV miniseries called *Million Dollar Babies* that I watched as a teenager. The two-part drama tells the story of their tumultuous young lives: five babies born to poor Ontario farmers, taken from their family, and exploited by the government. The Dionnes led what seemed to me a fairy-tale life. They were global celebrities just for being born. There were even villains and heroes in their story—Dr. Dafoe versus the girls' father, Oliva Dionne.

Many years after I watched the movie, sometime in the early 2000s, my husband and I were visiting his brother in North Bay, Ontario. We were driving on the highway when I noticed a sign that said, "Dionne Quints Museum." I suggested we take the exit. The house the quints had been born in had been moved from its original site and sat in a lonely, eerily quiet parking lot. That day, we were the only people around. The house was small and ordinary. It was a tidy farmhouse with a steep roof and a covered porch that wrapped around two sides of the home. We peered in the windows, but there wasn't much to see. Still, it made me feel sad. Their story had started there. The sight of the house, abandoned and lonely, was a telltale end to the family's story. It felt both heartbreaking and inevitable.

The Dionne Quints Museum closed in 2015 after operating for thirty years. Visitor attendance was low, and funding ran out. In 2017, the house was moved to another North Bay location on the city's waterfront. The two surviving quintuplets, Cecile and Annette, who were eighty-three in 2017, told CBC's *The National* that they hoped the government would provide funding to preserve their family home as a symbol of their story. They said people should know the toll exploitation took on them and their sisters, and what they still saw as a stolen childhood. The two sisters reminisced in the interview about how they once received countless birthday cards each year from around the world, but that year they had only received six. The sisters were on site at the home's new location for a plaque dedication in 2018. It was the first time they'd been in their family home in twenty years.

There are several similarities and points of comparison between the Murray and Dionne stories. Both mothers had previous children, and the families were poor farmers. Both had lost kids to illness. Although little is documented in the Murray quintuplets' birth, we do know there was a midwife there and then later a doctor. They may have played out similarly. And though the story of the Murray quints is necessarily short—as were their lives—there is another key point of similarity between the Murray babies and the Dionne sisters: the mix of prurient public interest and a willing facilitator. In the case of the Dionne quintuplets, Oliva Dionne, and then the province of Ontario and Dr. Dafoe were willing to put the lives of the children on display for the public. In the case of the Murray quintuplets, the biggest showman of the day was keen to exploit the family's tragedy.

I do wonder what might have happened if Adam and Maria had decided to sell the bodies of their babies to P. T. Barnum. The Murrays were poor, and the money was likely a tempting option (as was the case with Mr. Dionne and the Chicago Fair). But the Murrays rejected the offer. Something held them back. Was it fear of exploitation? A moral consciousness? Shame? Parental protectiveness? Or perhaps they were just simple farm folks who did not wish to be in the spotlight.

If the Murray family had sold the bodies of their dead children, would the Murrays have become famous? The year 1880 was a time when a curiosity like five dead infants would have been a popular circus attraction. Could these deceased children have put Pictou County and Little Egypt on the world stage? Would their place of birth or burial have a monument of some kind today, instead of being an unknown, unmarked, forgotten location? And consider the opposite for the Dionne quintuplets. If they had been kept out of the spotlight and allowed to live normal lives, would they have been happier?

In an April 9, 1880, article about the miraculous Murray quintuplet birth in the *Cincinnati Daily Star*, the headline read: "Mrs. Murray produced 'A Litter of Babies.'" Could embarrassment be one of the reasons the babies were so seldom talked about within the Murray family and the reason there was practically nothing written about them after their deaths? Perhaps like the Dionne family, and the mother in the fictional Grimm fairy tale, they worried about the judgement of others.

There are other known multiple births with similarities to both the Murray and Dionne experiences. The first American quintuplets on record is one of them.

The Lyon quintuplets were born on April 29, 1896, near Mayfield, Kentucky, to Elizabeth and Oscar Lyon. The family was living on a thirty-acre tobacco farm in a small three-room farmhouse. They had six children ranging in age from two to twenty. Elizabeth, a tiny woman at thirty-nine years old, was experiencing her eighth pregnancy; she had lost a child years before due to illness.

Elizabeth gave birth to five seemingly healthy boys without complications. One placenta and five cords meant the boys were identical. The babies were decent sizes for multiples, all weighing between 3 and 4¼ pounds. Given how healthy they were at birth, the doctor expected the boys to live. They were given Biblical names: Matthew, Mark, Luke, John, and Paul.

The Lyon home was located near the Illinois Central Railroad tracks, and passenger trains began stopping there when news of the quints got out. Special trains came from as far away as Chicago.

Thousands of people came to see the miracle birth. At one point the Lyons started charging people to see the babies and made a total of $600 (the equivalent of about $18,000 US today). So many people came that police eventually had to stand guard to keep them from forcing their way into the home.

At this time, feeding infants bottled milk was frowned upon. Elizabeth was breastfeeding the babies, and even though she had the help of a wet nurse, the babies were not gaining weight. They were described as "becoming emaciated."

The family had offers from people looking to "borrow" or "rent" the miracle children. The *Sentinel* newspaper in Carlisle, Pennsylvania, reported on May 6, 1896, that "one man offered them $10,000 for a limited number of months." At the time, it was reported in the papers that "the children are all doing nicely." This wasn't in fact true, as one of the babies had died on May 4; the others followed on May 11, 12, 13, and 14.

The *Akron Beacon* printed on May 28, 1896: "All the [Lyon] quintuplets dead.... In each case death was sudden, each little victim giving a scream as it expired." The infants were believed to have died due to starvation.

The Lyon family purchased a plot for their sons in a local cemetery, but with so much public interest—and commercial interest—in the babies, the family feared grave robbers and decided against burying them. Then it became a situation of what to do with the bodies. The embalmed Lyon babies were temporarily on display at the undertaking parlour until the embalming service was paid for, as the family struggled to come up with the money. There was a picture taken of the dead quintuplets alongside their parents. In the old sepia-toned photo, the babies are dressed in white baptismal-style dresses and laid out on a white background in a glass, coffin-like case. Their eyes appear dark and open, although I'm sure they would have been closed by the undertaker. The faces of the parents are solemn. Oscar Lyon wore a formal suit over his tall, thin frame. His moustache was neat. Elizabeth was dressed in a long puff-sleeved black dress that covered her neck and wrists.

The Lyons had the bodies on display for a time in their home. The buzz around the rare birth continued for a time, and stories were published all over the world. The *Reynold's Newspaper* of London, England, ran a story in its August 23, 1896, edition: "Mr. and Mrs. Lyon, a pair in very humble circumstances, recently had five children. The babes died and were embalmed. Now they are in a showcase, and the whole family is exhibited for ten cents." The family was in a difficult financial situation and, given their circumstances, the parents were forced to continue showing their dead children for as long as there was public interest. Eventually, the embalmed bodies ended up with a local doctor. He had them mummified and kept in a display case, which he took to county fairs for years.

In 1905, the bodies of the quints were returned to the Lyons once more. They kept them for a time but were uncertain what to do with them. The family's financial situation had not improved, and they were getting older. Mrs. Lyon contacted the National Museum of Health and Medicine, established in Washington, DC, during the Civil War as an army medical museum for the collection of specimens for research in military medicine, and attempted to sell the mummified bodies for $1,500. She wanted them to be used for education and science. The museum declined her offer but, in the end, paid the family $100 for them. Elizabeth sent them to the museum packed in newspaper.

When the Dionne quintuplets were born in 1934, Mrs. Lyon spoke out publicly with warnings to the family. She claimed it was the crowds that killed her babies. At age seventy-eight, she warned Mrs. Dionne not to make the same mistake. On June 2, 1943, the *Messenger-Inquirer* of Owensboro, Kentucky, quoted Mrs. Lyon: "I'm going to write to this mother in Canada and tell her what to do. I'm going to tell her to keep everybody away from those babies of hers; if she doesn't she will lose them all."

Although they are no longer on display, the bodies of the Lyon quintuplets have been part of past exhibits at the National Museum of Health and Medicine (previously known as the Army Medical Museum in Washington, DC). When the museum reopened to the public in Washington in 1978, the five little bodies were displayed amongst some ill-fated medical rarities, including a one-eyed baby; a fetus with legs fused together to form what looked like a mermaid tail; President Lincoln's hair and a small piece of his bone; and John Wilkes Booth's vertebrae, complete with bullet hole.

Other multiples have lived relatively normal lives. Consider quintuplets born to Franco Diligenti and opera singer Ana Aversano in Argentina in 1943. They had a very different upbringing from the Dionnes. Determined to protect their children from "circus-like" publicity, the couple kept the birth quiet. Mr. Diligenti refused to let any news reporters see the quints—three girls and two boys (the same as the Murrays)—and kept them as much out of the limelight as possible. Diligenti, a successful businessman, sent each of the quintuplets to a different boarding school so they learned to be individuals. The children had relatively normal upbringings and went on to live successful lives.

Although not as rare as quintuplets, quadruplets were still a celebrated phenomenon. In 1923, the Mahaney quadruplets—three girls and one boy—were born on Christmas Day in Saint John, New Brunswick. The children had fairly average, happy childhoods, and they were quite popular in Canadian media before the Dionnes were born. Although there were other recorded births of quadruplets in North America, the Mahaneys were commonly featured in newspapers and on postcards as "Canada's only living quads." There's a December 27, 1935, news clipping with a picture of the Mahaney quads reading a telegram that said a cash gift was on the way from the guardians of the Dionne quintuplets "to assure them a happy Christmas."

This longtime fascination with multiples is still a form of entertainment today. Their stories are made even more popular due to the common use of fertility drugs that became widely available in the 1990s. For example, in 1988, there were 229 sets of quads and 40 sets of quints born in the United States; in 2006, the statistics were 355 and 67.

People are naturally curious about how a family can manage with multiples. Typically, with big families, the older children will help with the younger ones. But how do two adults look after five infants or toddlers alone? The basic logistics of it seem impossible. They would be forever changing diapers and preparing bottles and giving baths. And when would one have time for sleep? Or work?

I'm not a fan of reality TV, but when the show *Jon & Kate Plus 8* first aired in 2007, I did watch a few episodes. The show followed Jon and Kate Gosselin of Hershey, Pennsylvania, and their eight children: a set of twins followed by sextuplets. Kate became pregnant both times with the help of fertility treatments. The family's lives were portrayed over eleven seasons, through childhood firsts, parenting squabbles, divorce, and then Kate as a single mother.

The family members' faces graced the covers of magazines for decades. *Quints by Surprise*, another popular show, followed Casey and Ethan Jones of Austin, Texas, and their six children, including quintuplets born in January 2009. All their children were conceived through artificial insemination. The TLC show followed their daily lives and aired the first of its four seasons in 2010. The list of media sensations goes on, including the controversial "Octomom" Nadya Suleman, who had six children and then octuplets through in-vitro pregnancies. She was a single mom living on public assistance who became a tabloid sensation.

Obviously, not all multiple-birth families become celebrities with TV shows and fancy lifestyles. What most families of multiples need more than fame are diapers, home-cooked meals, and a helping hand. However, given the high cost of raising a child in Canada, one can understand the appeal. The average cost ranges from $12,000 to $15,000 per year, amounting to a minimum of $216,000 over eighteen years. When multiplied by five, the total is $1,080,000. It's clear why the option of having a TV crew follow you around a few days a week would be tempting, even if it resulted in turning your home into a bit of a circus act for all the world to see. Like the curiosities of a nineteenth- and early twentieth-century sideshow, it's a price some are willing to pay for fame and fortune, or simply for survival.

LITTLE EGYPT 1950S: A GHOST, A WEDDING, AND THE LIFE THAT FOLLOWED

Annie saw something strange out behind her house late one night. It was a white, cloud-like entity that floated through her dark yard and across the field before it disappeared into the woods.

She was normally a level-headed person, and even though she knew she would sound crazy, she had to tell someone. The next morning, she gathered the girls and ran across the fields to the Murray farmhouse.

"I saw a ghost," she told Uncle Jim, and then went on to explain what she had seen.

Uncle Jim laughed. No, he told her, that was one of the boys from the neighbouring farm. Jim had caught the kid stealing one of his chickens. The boy had it in a white pillowcase, and what Annie saw was the chicken trying madly to escape as the boy made a run for it.

Thieving had become a serious problem out on the farm. The stealing had gotten so bad Jim moved his main vegetable garden to the back field to keep the thieves from helping themselves to all of his crop.

Annie recognized that Jim's story made perfect sense, and they laughed over her error. But ghost or no ghost, the sight of the boy and the pillowcase had given Annie a fright. She was still nervous after the shooting incident, and she was tired of living alone.

When Annie met Frederick Brown in the summer of 1945, she felt her unlucky life was finally about to change. Raising her daughters on her own these past seven years had been challenging, both financially and emotionally.

Fred wasn't a resident of Pictou County but had landed there by chance, as he had taken a job at the Trenton Steel Works as a high rigger. The plant was replacing all the high windows in the buildings, and finding someone willing to climb the tall ladders wasn't an easy job. Fred wasn't afraid of heights and spent most of that summer at the top of dangerous scaffoldings and ladders.

Fred, at fifty-two, was twenty-three years older than Annie, who was twenty-nine. He was tall, with thinning brown hair and kind eyes. Annie thought he had a distinguished way about him, even though he was wearing dirty workman's coveralls the day they happened to meet at a shop in Trenton.

Fred was originally from Boylston, a small town in Guysborough County, Nova Scotia, and had lived out west for many years after serving in the war. He was divorced and had just moved back to the province. He was only in Trenton temporarily for work. He told Annie that if she could give him a reason to stay, he would.

There was no lengthy dating period. Annie was looking for someone who would be a good provider for her and her girls, and she had found that someone in Fred. The couple were married at a parsonage in New Glasgow with little fanfare, and Fred immediately moved into the guest house with them. Doris was still living in Trenton with her grandparents, but Ginger and Phyllis, who were nine and ten at the time, loved having their new stepfather in the house. He was kind, he loved to bake, and he even built them a playhouse. They actually had money for the first time in their lives. And best of all, Fred had a car.

The girls loved going for long drives, especially to Boylston, where they went to visit his family. The car had a rumble seat in the back that popped up for extra passengers, and Ginger and Phyllis would pile in the back. The car had no top, so drives could be dusty on the old back roads, but they didn't care.

Fred was a hard worker and was handy at a lot of trades, including carpentry, plumbing, and electrical work. When he wasn't working for some local company that needed him for an odd job, he helped Uncle Jim on the farm.

Fred immediately set about making life better for his new family. The first thing he did was buy a piece of land farther up the Little Egypt Road. He wanted them to have a house with electricity and indoor plumbing; the chemical toilet they used in winter and the outhouse were far from ideal. Fred also wanted a place that was closer to school. Annie was paying one of her sisters to let Ginger board through the week so she didn't have to walk all the way to school by herself, but Ginger was unhappy being away from her family.

A few years after they were married, Annie became pregnant.

Ginger, who was twelve at the time, was horrified. Her mother, she thought, was too old at thirty-three to be having a baby. She didn't tell any of her friends and refused to talk about it to anyone. But once the baby was born—a girl they named Twila, who would become my mother—Ginger was enamoured. The baby was like a little doll she could dress up and take places.

Not long after Twila was born, the family moved into their new home farther up the Little Egypt Road. The year was 1950. It was a modern house with three bedrooms, beautiful hardwood floors, and an inside bathroom with a tin shower that the girls thought made a delightful sound when they used it. Doris stayed at her grandparents' place in Trenton. It had become her home.

A few weeks after they'd vacated the guest house on the Murray farm, someone came onto the property in the middle of the night and set the little house on fire, burning it to the ground. The Murrays didn't know who did it, or if they did, they had no way to prove it. There was someone in the area who liked to intentionally set fires and the guest house was just one of many casualties in the area at the time.

As the years went on, Phyllis's seizures continued, and she became more and more agitated. Playing cards and doing puzzles didn't placate her the way they had in the past. Although never mean-spirited, Phyllis could become violent when she was having one of her bad days. Annie knew something had to change.

The only solution available to them was to send Phyllis to an institution. When she was in her late teens, Phyllis moved to the Nova Scotia Hospital, a large psychiatric facility in Dartmouth. She liked most aspects of her new life away from home, but had to endure periodic treatments involving electroshock therapy. The electrically induced seizures provided her with temporary relief from her mental anguish, but Phyllis hated it because it was painful and left her groggy for days.

Annie missed Phyllis dearly, and at the same time felt exhausted trying to raise another young daughter. She didn't have the patience she'd once had for children and she and Fred argued often. Her years of solitude on the farm had made her difficult to live with, and at times their vast age difference caught up with them. They were very different. Some days, Fred found it best to just stay out of her way. He would travel to Guysborough to visit his family, or he would spend long stretches of time living on the Murray farm, helping Annie's aunts and uncles.

Fred was a veteran of the First World War and had served three years on the front line. He had gone into battle with more than 2,000 men in his battalion and was one of only 190 to survive. He suffered from what was then called "shell shock" (we know it now as PTSD) and sometimes had trouble sleeping. He would often be quiet for long stretches of time. He also had some health problems from the war, including a shrunken bladder from being severely dehydrated, and problems with his lungs from gas exposure. He never complained. If he had, Annie would have had no empathy for him. She had none left to give.

LITTLE EGYPT, 1880: THE COMMUNITY VISITS

Early on Monday, February 16, 1880, the day following the quintuplets' birth, a fourth baby died. Only little Jeanette was still alive. Hearing of the four deaths, a neighbour built a small rosewood casket and sent it over to Adam and Maria's home.

Other members of the local community and beyond started asking if they could see the wonder that was the five babies. Unaccustomed to the attention they were receiving, Maria and Adam were hesitant to let strangers into their home. But they were also in a desperate financial situation and in need of the community's support. Winter was difficult on the Little Egypt farm. Fresh food was scarce. They knew if people came, they would bring money and gifts. Every little bit helped, so the family resigned themselves to visitors.

John R. P. Fraser's photo of the bodies of four of the quintuplets—Elizabeth, Margaret, James, and William, all lined up snugly.

The quintuplets needed to be presentable and were dressed in identical little white christening dresses, a gift sent to them from someone in town. The bodies of Elizabeth, Margaret, James, and William were laid out in the plain little rosewood coffin.

They lined up snugly.

People began arriving at the home late in the morning on Monday, February 16. They came from the nearby rural communities, plus the towns of New Glasgow, Stellarton, Westville, and Pictou. Hundreds of curious people came to pay their respects and to sneak a peek at the local phenomenon.

One such guest, according to a personal account in the *Calgary Herald* (June 6, 1934), was Myra MacKenzie. Myra, a child at the time, had met Mr. Murray on more than one occasion at her grandmother's place—Mrs. Isabelle MacKay's in New Glasgow. Mr. Murray did odd jobs around the house for the family. (She recalled: "The family, together with all the residents of the countryside, were deeply interested in the welfare of the parents, who had several children before the advent of the quintuplets and were practically destitute.... No one had ever heard tell of such a thing before, and it caused a great sensation. Everyone did what they could to help the parents.")

As Myra stepped into the Murray farmhouse, she likely looked around in awe. She had probably never been in a house like this one before. She looked with fascination not only at the quintuplets, who were laid out like beautiful little dolls, but also at the family and their home itself.

The Murray children were dressed in what would have been their best clothing, but as the family did not attend church regularly, they probably had little to choose from. Myra was, perhaps, wondering what else her family could do to help them.

Even travellers from beyond Pictou County made a point of visiting. (The *Morning Journal-Courier* of New Haven Connecticut reported this account on March 13, 1880: "The *Hartford Times* of yesterday says: We are indebted to Constable Phelps, of this city, for a copy of the *Colonial Standard*, published at Pictou, Nova Scotia, containing an account of five babies at one birth. Mr. Phelps, who was on a visit to Nova Scotia, saw the babies after death.")

The exchange between strangers and the family would have been cordial but understandably awkward. Condolences as well as congratulations. As the guests gazed at the infants, they called them "positively beautiful" and "like little cherubs." One guest later referred to "the dead ones resembling works of art in wax [rather] than natural-born members of our race." Little Jeanette was proudly held by family members. She was admired as all newborns are, with oohs and aahs.

Little Egypt had never been in the spotlight before in such a way, nor would it ever be again.

CHAPTER 9: RITUALS OF DEATH

Everyone remembers the first dead body they ever saw. Mine was my grandfather, Fred Brown. He was eighty-seven when he died. I was seven. I remember it clearly. My parents took me and my six-year-old brother for a private viewing before the funeral home was open for visitation. It was just us in the room with the casket. My grandfather was dressed in a navy suit and a red tie. His hands were folded neatly at the bottom of his chest. They looked glued together. I remember reaching out and touching his fingers. His skin felt like hard wax. I also recall the smell of the flowers that surrounded him. Back then, people sent flowers to show their compassion instead of the more modern custom of a charitable donation, and my grandfather was encircled by them.

Fred lived his last years at a veteran's long-term care facility in Halifax called Camp Hill. The facility still provides care to more than one hundred veterans, but as the number of living war veterans declines, it has also become home to other seniors who can no longer care for themselves. At the time, my grandfather didn't actually need the level of care they offered, as he was still healthy enough to walk fifteen kilometres each day. There was simply nowhere else that was suitable for his other medical needs.

I have vague memories of visiting him there. He was a tall, thin man with pale, wrinkled skin. His head was mostly bald, with thin fluffs of white hair on the sides. His eyes crinkled behind black-framed glasses. Sometimes he smiled with no teeth.

My grandmother would make weekly trips to Halifax to visit Phyllis at the Nova Scotia Hospital. Occasionally, out of a sense of duty, she would also visit her estranged husband at Camp Hill. Sometimes I would go with her, or my parents would drive us all up for a Sunday afternoon visit. My grandparents had lived apart for decades at this point. I imagine them sitting in his room at Camp Hill in uncomfortable silence, him staring up at the ceiling and her in the adjacent chair eating pink peppermints and reading the *National Enquirer* until it was time for her to leave.

Although I remember precious little about my grandfather, my mother tells me he was an exceptionally good man. The sort of man who took on stepchildren as if they were his own. The sort of man who built his young wife her dream home and paid for everything.

When Fred died, Annie was by his side at the funeral home. There were no tears, but that didn't mean she wasn't sad. I don't think I ever saw my grandmother cry. I once asked her if she missed either of her husbands; she simply shrugged. I think the hardships she'd experienced as a young mother alone on the Murray farm left her impenetrable. Grammie once told one of my cousins she never got to spend her life with the man she loved. Who that was, we'll never know. She didn't elaborate.

My grandfather's remains were held at R. H. Porter Funeral Home, which is in a modified old house in New Glasgow. "House" isn't exactly the right word; it looks more like a gloomy but elegant medieval castle. It was one of the town's first great homes and is rumoured to have a secret rum-runner's tunnel beneath it that leads to the East River. Coincidentally, this funeral parlour is located directly across the road from my husband's childhood home. He says it gave him nightmares as a child.

When my grandfather's remains were at Porter's in 1987, funeral director Bob Porter—a friendly man with a truly sympathetic smile—offered me and my brother a once-in-a-lifetime invitation. "Would you like a tour of the funeral home?" he asked.

I have been in this particular funeral home many times over the years and appreciate the timelessness of the beautiful wood staircase, cabinets, and detailing; the elaborate old fireplaces; and the creepy basement family sitting room (where the wood walls and ceiling make you feel like you're six feet under), but the only thing I remember from that childhood tour is the casket room he showed us.

One of the upstairs bedrooms was used for display caskets. In my memory, he took us to the round room at the very top of the house. (I like the image I have of this tour and have no plans to fact-check this.) The room was filled with a selection of caskets for purchase. They were available in a variety of woods, metals, colours, sizes, and price points. My brother and I ran around them. We each picked out the casket we wanted to be buried in. We laughed. It was fun.

A child sees death and experiences grief far differently than an adult does. To them, it's something far off. Their mortality is something they don't yet recognize. I remember my mother's red-rimmed eyes when she broke the news to me about her father's passing. I think she expected me to be more upset than I was. Although I understood he was gone and would not be coming back, I was too young to understand the grief she felt at losing her father. Children grow up with stories of death disguised in fairy tales. Little Red Riding Hood's grandmother is swallowed whole by a wolf, the cannibalistic old woman in Hansel and Gretel is cooked in her own fiery oven, the witch at the end of Snow White falls to her well-deserved death. To the young, they're just stories. This all changes when someone, young or old, faces a loss first-hand.

It wasn't just Adam and Maria who experienced the death of the quintuplets back in 1880; their children did as well. Some of the older kids would have remembered losing their three siblings to diphtheria in 1875. Were those deaths still raw to them? The loss of these new siblings would, of course, be different. These infants had never brightened a room with first smiles or kept everyone up crying through the night. The older kids wouldn't have had to share toys or help with feedings. Poor farm children of that time would have had a different relationship with siblings than I had with my one brother growing up in a comfortable middle-class family in the 1980s and '90s. The Murray children likely helped look after their younger siblings day and night, in addition to regular farm chores. It was just the way it was.

In 1880, the infant and child mortality rates were high. The odds of a child dying before his or her fifth birthday was around 20 percent. A walk through an old Nova Scotia cemetery will show dates of many deceased children from the eighteenth, nineteenth, and even the early twentieth centuries. Some children have a headstone of their own, often with a lamb or rocking horse engraved at the top; others will just have a marker in front of their parents' graves. Many parents were predeceased by more than one child.

There's a museum in Halifax called Evergreen House that once belonged to provincial court judge Alexander James and his wife, Harriet Hawthorn. The couple lost eight children to diphtheria in 1858. After the tragedy, Mr. James had a beautiful home built (Evergreen House) so he, his wife, and their three remaining children could start a new life. This home, now part of the Dartmouth Heritage Museum, overlooks Halifax Harbour. Its location is considered part of the city now, but back then, it would have been countryside. Dr. Helen Creighton, one of Canada's best-known folklorists, also lived in the home. I've visited the museum many times over the years; I love the history and atmosphere of the place. There's a room at the back that offers a panoramic view. When I last visited, Dr. Creighton's old typewriter and writing desk were on display in the room. I imagined her sitting there, inspired by her surroundings—the lovely view, the wonderful old house, and the memory of the Jameses' lost children—as she wrote her famous local ghost stories.

Although families would have understood the risks facing young children in the nineteenth century, it would not have made death any easier to accept. I love this quote by author Jamie Anderson about grief: "Grief, I've learned, is really just love. It's all the love you want to give, but cannot. All that unspent love gathers up in the corners of your eyes, the lump in your throat, and in that hollow part of your chest. Grief is just love with no place to go."

Some people, as they age, begin planning their own death rituals. Grammie had her funeral planned and her casket and burial plot paid for decades before she died. She also had everything arranged for her daughter Phyllis and her sister Ethel. All three are now together at Heatherdale Memorial Gardens in Pictou, buried in neighbouring plots. When the topic of death comes up in conversation, people will often make their wishes known. My mother is always quick to say she wants to be cremated. "Don't put me in the ground!" she insists. I, on the other hand, find the idea of cremation horrifying. But embalming sounds almost as bad.

I tell people I'd like a green burial. Dress me up in something nice and bury me in a compostable wooden box. Maybe plant a nice lilac or willow tree above me. I've done some research and found out there's a local movement in Nova Scotia toward this kind of burial. It seems there are others who share similar feelings; they're looking for something natural in this synthetic world of ours. However, many people have never even heard of it.

While it may seem like I dwell on the topic of death, I want to clarify that I don't. It doesn't occupy any more time in my mind than the average person's. The difference is that I'm not afraid to talk about it, where it makes many others uncomfortable. Death, to me, is more of an abstract concept—a notion that both unsettles and fascinates me. It represents the ultimate mystery. I believe discussing death openly and honestly is essential for fostering greater acceptance, understanding, and preparation for the inevitable.

We know about past societies because of how they buried their dead. What does it say about our world today, where cremation is the norm? What are we leaving behind except scattered ashes and urns on mantels?

Some of the most remarkable burial traditions involve the ancient Egyptians and their mummies and elaborate tombs. We know they worshipped and memorialized their dead kings and queens. The ancient Tibetans practised a vastly different type of burial known as a sky burial, where a corpse would be left on a mountain and open to the elements and wildlife, in particular birds of prey. Some modern practices are even more unconventional. There is now something called extreme embalming. It's a practice done occasionally in various places around the world, such as Louisiana and Puerto Rico, where the deceased is propped up and displayed like a wax figure in a museum. They may be sitting in their favourite chair, at a table with a beer, playing a video game, or straddling their motorbike. Like a taxidermized animal, they are presented in death as they were in life. Bodies are preserved with a strong chemical fluid that makes them rigid. The undertaker will use poles and nails to form the corpse's fixed position. With a lot of makeup and the right clothes, the deceased is able to attend their own funeral, in a very bizarre way, instead of being on display in a traditional casket.

Although practices vary vastly from religion to religion, culture to culture, and person to person, it is typical in North America to have three rituals of mourning: the visitation, the funeral, and the burial (in a graveyard/cemetery) or a scattering of ashes. In the seventeenth, eighteenth, and nineteenth centuries, the family, friends, and neighbours of the deceased would hold the visitation at home. Funeral parlours came into the picture at the end of the nineteenth century, taking the organizational burden off the family after a death, but the hosting of remains in a family home was still customary for many decades after.

There were countless family funeral visitations held at our Murray farm over the years. Aunt Doris remembers one of her old aunts laid out in the living room in the 1940s. "She was the first dead person I ever saw," Doris recalled. "My mother said to me, 'Now, go give Aunt Niney a final kiss.' I walked up to the casket, and I did as I was told. I'll always remember the way she felt. It was the one and only time I ever did that."

The hosting of a family member's remains in the home continued to be common practice for another thirty years after that. My mother remembers her Great-Aunt Libby's visitation in the living room of her mother's place in Trenton in 1962, Libby being one of the last inhabitants of the Murray farm.

The oldest funeral home in Halifax is J. A. Snow Funeral Home, which opened in 1883. They were the undertakers who looked after the *Titanic* bodies when they were brought ashore during Halifax's rescue and recovery efforts in 1912. Many of these bodies are buried in Halifax cemeteries, some with names unknown. Snow's also looked after the approximately two thousand bodies of the Halifax Explosion in the winter of 1917, a result of a collision in the Halifax Harbour between a French munitions ship, the SS *Mont Blanc*, and the Norwegian vessel, the SS *Imo*, that levelled a large portion of the city.

I thought Snow's, as the city's oldest funeral home, might have some insight into burial practices of the 1880s. I arranged a visit with Don MacKay, a staff member with fifty-plus years in the business.

When I arrived at the funeral home for our interview, there was a memorial service about to start. The parking lot was full, and groups of chatting mourners gathered at the door. I waited a moment in my car, unsure of the etiquette. Should I just walk right in? I felt like a funeral crasher. But I also didn't want to be late, so I eventually made my way to the door. I kept my head down to avoid eye contact with the grievers. Don was waiting for me just inside. He reassured me my being there was just fine, and I felt immediately comfortable.

We sat in what they call The Titanic room; it has pictures on the wall of navy boats and an iceberg, which were taken during the unsinkable ship's search and rescue. As we got settled at the table, I gave him a quick overview of my project. He, like almost everyone I'd encountered in my search, had not heard the story of the Murray quintuplets, and made a point of telling me anything he had to offer was 100 percent speculation.

The first topic up for discussion: embalming.

"Do you think they would have embalmed the babies back in 1880?" I asked.

He pondered my question a moment. "It's unlikely," he offered, "but possible. It depended on what the family wanted. If I were to guess, I would say no. They were just tiny babies, after all."

Embalming became common in North America during the time of the American Civil War. When troops from the North were killed in the South, they needed to be preserved. Thomas H. Holmes, MD, started the medical specialty of embalming in 1863. He and his colleagues embalmed and shipped soldiers' bodies. It cost $100 for officers and $25 for enlisted men. After the war, he claimed to have embalmed 4,028 men.

Embalming fluids are typically a mixture of formaldehyde, glutaraldehyde, and methanol. Modern undertakers use a machine to drain the blood from the arteries and replace it with embalming fluid, which temporarily prevents decomposition.

Embalming is the norm in North America today. The US alone uses approximately 20 million litres of embalming fluid each year. Most undertakers wouldn't even consider offering a viewing of a body unless it was first embalmed, so if you think a body becomes "worm food" right away, you're mistaken. Depending on the state of the body at the time of burial, the temperature, and the type of casket and vault, the body can take decades to decompose. A body that is buried six feet under with no embalming decomposes much more quickly (several weeks to months, depending on environmental factors).

I asked Don if he thought cost may have been a factor in deciding about the embalming of the quintuplets, as the Murrays had no money for extras of any kind.

"Given what I know about the old days and going back to the history of Snow's, a lot of these old undertakers wouldn't have charged people anything for embalming a baby. Even today, young couples starting out will lose a baby and the funeral home will often waive the charges."

Don remembers that when Snow's was in its original location in downtown Halifax on Argyle Street, they had all the cases of embalming equipment set up to transport for home embalming, which was done often back in the day. (That same Argyle Street building is currently home to a popular Halifax restaurant that is said to be one of the most haunted buildings in Canada!)

Don added that many of the early settlers in rural areas would bury their family members right on their property. And if that was the case, embalming was even less likely. As communities became more established, so too did local cemeteries. But for many years, the nearby woods or the backyard were final resting places.

"Today, when people are looking to buy a piece of rural property and walk along the grounds, they'll sometimes come across a monument of some kind and realize someone is buried there," said Don.

He told me it's still permissible to bury a body on private property in most Canadian provinces so long as certain requirements are met. For example, there can't be any public health concerns, such as being too close to a well, and you would have to check the zoning, acquire a permit from the local authority, and notify the Land Registry. It isn't a common practice, for various and obvious reasons.

"It's fine if you're in a situation where you're living there, but if you go to sell the property, you'll have to disclose that the body is there," said Don. "If I'm coming to buy a piece of land from you and you tell me there's a body or burial ground in the backyard, that may be all it takes to discourage me from buying. Or you'd have to make arrangements to have the body exhumed and moved."

I thought of a friend who had recently dug up their dead cat from their backyard when they moved to a new home. Not wanting to leave him behind, they reburied him in their new backyard.

My next question for Don was about the burial itself. I explained how each of the Murray quintuplets died at different times, and that it was believed four babies were buried together and the fifth baby on the following day. Did that mean Jeanette, the fifth baby, had her own rosewood casket, I wondered? Or did they dig up the other one and add her in? Or maybe each baby had a little rosewood casket of his or her own?

"It's hard to say what they would have done. In today's world there would be a casket for each. And it wouldn't surprise me if there were individual infant caskets back then, given how common infant mortality was. But this family lost five at one time, so that's different."

I learned from a local newspaper article that the Murray family had a casket for four of the quintuplets, which was a gift from a neighbour. Undertaking, as a profession, was a respectable livelihood for individuals in the 1880s. A fabric-lined casket with a glass cover could be purchased for a standard price of ten dollars. A more extravagant coffin with a black broadcloth covering could be bought for thirty dollars. Undertakers also offered hearses drawn with horses. Today, the price of a traditional funeral in Nova Scotia is about $10,000, but it can cost much more, depending on personal preferences.

It's interesting to note that the newspaper articles about the Murray quintuplets used the word *casket* not *coffin*. There is a picture of the four dead babies lined up in a little box, which may or may not have been the actual casket. One newspaper article referred to it as a "rosewood box," and I think this is a good possibility.

A casket, by definition, is a fancier coffin. It is rectangular in shape with four sides, a top, and a bottom, whereas a coffin has a hexagon shape with wider shoulders. Caskets are typically lined inside with padded mattresses and pillows, characteristics not evident in the picture I found at the Carmichael-Stewart House Museum. That box is very plain. It appears light in colour, but while classic rosewood is dark to reddish-brown, there are lighter variations as well, depending on the species of wood. Because rosewood is not native to Canada, it would have been imported from somewhere—possibly Africa, Southeast Asia, or India—making the gift extravagant and expensive. Rosewood may also have been the wood of choice to help mask the smell of the bodies, particularly if they had not been embalmed. The popular wood was known for its scent and often used in oils and perfumes. Due to its overuse in luxury items such as flooring, furniture, musical instruments, and caskets, rosewood is now considered an endangered species and the trees are protected worldwide.

I was also curious about the time of year for the burial itself. Today, it is common for a body to be kept in a winter vault until the ground thaws for a spring interment. I figured they couldn't possibly have had means to bury bodies in the frozen ground back in the nineteenth century. Don assured me otherwise.

"Oh, they would have definitely buried them," he said. "Waiting for the ground to thaw is actually a relatively recent practice. When I first started, we did all our burials year-round. Then, eventually, they started constructing receiving vaults [a tomb designed to temporarily store dead bodies in winter], which always surprised me. They didn't even have the equipment back then that we have now."

He then asked me something I hadn't thought of before. "Were the babies baptized?"

I had no idea.

Adam and Maria Murray's marriage certificate states they were members of the Church of Scotland, the Presbyterian faith of many of the Scottish settlers. The few articles and short stories about the quintuplets all note visits from the neighbours, the townspeople, the photographer, and the undertaker, but none mentions a minister, although given the culture of the time, baptisms would have been normal and considered vital. In comparison, the Dionne quintuplets were baptized by the Catholic midwives immediately after their tiny, frail bodies entered the world.

"I haven't found any record of them being baptized," I told him. "But there was a funeral."

The funeral's date and time was noted in the local newspaper. Although the location was not named, it can be assumed the funeral was held at what is currently St. Andrew's Presbyterian Church in New Glasgow. The church was founded in 1819, and the current building was built in 1856. It has always been known as the Kirk on the Hill, or the Kirk church ("the Kirk" being another name for the Church of Scotland). This was my Murray ancestors' family church back in the late nineteenth century, and they attended when they could.

Doris has been going to the Kirk church for almost fifty years. By looking through old baptism records, she found her grandfather Andrew Murray's baptism, as well as some—but not all—of his siblings, who were born in or near the 1880s. There is no record of any of Adam and Maria's children in the church archives.

The church's location may have been a factor in the family's poor church attendance record, as it is located in New Glasgow and a good distance from Little Egypt, which was made even more problematic by their lack of adequate transportation. From what my mother remembers, her grandfather and great-aunts and -uncles on the farm didn't attend church every Sunday, but they did pay into a church. Doris remembers her grandfather (Andrew) telling her about a time he walked through the woods to the church as a boy. He and his father (John) apparently walked the entire way carrying their shoes so as to keep them clean, and only put them on when they entered the building. It was a memorable event for him, which makes one think he didn't do it often.

Don and I ended our interview at the funeral home with a brief chat about people he thought may have direct answers to my questions. Unfortunately, all of them had passed away. This, I explained, did not surprise me.

"It's an obstacle I'm constantly running into," I told him. "If only I'd started writing this story a decade or so earlier."

Don offered to ask around to see if he could find out anything, which I appreciated, then he walked me to the door. The service that had been going on when I came in was now over and the place was empty and silent. For that mourning family, it was time to move onto the next and final stage of the rituals of death—the burial.

LITTLE EGYPT 1880: THE PHOTOGRAPHER VISITS

John R. P. Fraser (no relation to Dr. Fraser "Downie") was a big man with inky black hair and an unkempt beard and moustache. As New Glasgow's first professional photographer, he was well-known and generally well liked. If someone didn't know him, they at least knew his name, as he advertised weekly in the *Eastern Chronicle*. He promoted his stand on Provost Street and his ad claimed: "He can give you as good work as can be done in the Province, as he has got an Artist to retouch his negatives in an artistic manner."

On the morning of Tuesday, February 17, 1880, two days after the quintuplets' birth, Mr. Fraser visited the Murray home.

The sight of the tiny dead infants would have been disconcerting, but Mr. Fraser was in awe. He would have known the photos he took that day would be important. (They were not only his most famous photos, but also among his last, as he became ill soon after and died later that year.)

Mr. Fraser took a few pictures of the dead infants. Someone had dressed and arranged them in a box (which may or may not have been their casket). They appeared to be sleeping. They were very still. Perfect. The family watched him. Given the circumstances, it was probably uncomfortably quiet.

He asked if he could take a photo of the five babies together: "the quintuplets." He had brought a staging pillow and satin blanket with him, as well as a background sheet, which he set up in the home. He propped the dead infants on the pillow—their bodies were stiff and awkward, and no one is comfortable handling a dead child. He adjusted and flattened their identical little white dresses, which were like the ones babies wore at the christenings and baptisms he photographed.

When everything was ready, he indicated someone in the family should hold the sleeping baby up beside them.

Then Mr. Fraser took his pictures.

At some point that same day the undertaker also stopped by. Although embalming was a common practice at the time, it is likely the mortician saw no need to embalm the infants, as they were to be buried the following day and had been kept near the cold front door when not on display for guests.

He measured and weighed each baby. The longest was 16 inches and 3 pounds, 14 ounces; the second was $15\frac{1}{4}$ inches and 3 pounds, 6 ounces; the third was $15\frac{1}{4}$ inches and 3 pounds, 4 ounces; and the fourth was $14\frac{5}{8}$ inches and 3 pounds. He also measured and weighed little Jeanette, who was alive. She measured 13½ inches and weighed 2 pounds, 8 ounces. The sizes were later recorded in the local newspaper.

The following day, Wednesday, February 18, 1880, four Murray babies were buried at the Riverside Cemetery near New Glasgow, overlooking the East River (as reported in the local newspaper). The cemetery dates back to the nineteenth century, with towering headstones and tall, ancient trees. It's the last resting place for some of the town's most prominent residents. The Murrays had no connection to this cemetery, and the burial plot may have been arranged by Dr. Fraser, who did have family buried there. The fee for the plot may have been waived or paid through donations. The babies might also have shared a plot with a recently deceased town resident whose family offered it, as this was sometimes the custom with infant deaths.

After the snowy graveyard burial, the family returned to their home in Little Egypt. Early that evening, regardless of all the love and hope the family and community showered on the last quintuplet, little Jeanette died.

Another rosewood casket was constructed and donated to the Murray family, and the next day, Jeanette Rankin Murray, the last surviving Murray quintuplet, was interred alongside her siblings.

One week after little Jeanette's death, the community held a funeral service for the Murray infants. It was held at 2:00 P.M. at the Kirk church in New Glasgow. The turnout of family, friends, and curious townspeople was substantial. A service for a child who died in infancy was not common, but this was a special situation. The Murray quintuplets made the town famous, if only for a short time.

LITTLE EGYPT, 1950S: THE LAST DAYS ON THE FARM

Out on the farm, life was becoming more and more difficult for the aging Murray siblings. Geordie passed away first, and then Jim died, leaving only Libby and Sarah.

Given her disability, Sarah had never lived anywhere but the farm. Her years had been spent playing with her dolls, all of whom were named Sweet Jean. Sarah wore plaid every single day and always had her hair cut and styled in the same boxy way, even though it was now grey. She didn't like change.

Libby didn't want to take Sarah away from her home on the farm. She sold off the animals and hired workers to come and cut the fields, but it was becoming too much for the women. Fred spent as much time as he could helping them.

One day, Twila was on the farm for a visit with her father. Her Great-Aunt Libby tried to give her a hug, but the little girl, age eight, squirmed just out of her reach. Libby fell to the floor of the farmhouse kitchen and broke her hip.

Unable to care for herself any longer, let alone the farm and Sarah, Libby was forced to leave the farm behind. Sarah was taken to a seniors' home nearby, where she was cared for until she passed away a few years later, and Libby went to live temporarily with Annie and Fred and the girls in Trenton. She died soon after.

Just like with Annie's guest house, a few weeks after Libby and Sarah's sudden move, someone came in the middle of the night and burned the old farmhouse to the ground. The arsonist—"fire-bug" was the term they used—was back. The culprit or culprits were never caught. The house that had been the Murray family homestead for generations, along with all its beautiful furniture and years of history—and possibly Uncle Jim's cash stashed in the walls—was gone.

CHAPTER 10:
MEMENTO MORI

I have a picture hanging in my home office of a young girl with dead eyes. It's a drawing on grey-blue paper in a grey-blue frame. She looks to be either a doll or a little girl dressed in old-fashioned clothing. She appears to be looking at nothing, but at the same time, right at you. Someone gave the picture to my mother, but she decided she didn't like it and added it to her yard sale box, which was where I found it.

"But don't you think it's creepy?" she asked me.

"Yeah, but I like creepy," I said.

I always have. Also in my office, in addition to hundreds of books and usually a cat or two, you'll find a small human-looking skull my son bought from a street vendor in Mexico (I have no idea of its origins, but it certainly looks real); a small statue of a corpse bride; an original oil painting of a dark and secluded cabin in the woods; and, naturally, a five-by-seven framed picture of the Murray quintuplets. I can't explain what draws me to things that are a bit dark. I guess I'd rather look at something unusual than something that's completely understood.

My interest in the Murray quintuplets began with that photo of the five babies that Mr. Fraser took. As a child, I would stare at

The author's grandmother, Annie, with her daughters Doris and Ginger.

the newspaper clipping in my grandmother's photo album, wondering where the bodies had ultimately been buried—were they in the cemetery still, or again? Or somewhere in woods behind the old farmhouse? It was this family secret—a mystery—I wanted to solve. I find most old photos can spark a sense of wonder. Black-and-white, nineteenth- and early twentieth-century photos portray a vastly different world than ours—and my imagination wants to time-travel, visit, poke around, inquire, learn, understand, marvel.

The author's great-grandfather, Andrew Murray.

I don't have many photos of my ancestors, but I probably have more than most people my age. I have a few pictures of my grandmother, Annie, as a young woman and photos of my mother and her sisters as children on the Murray farm. I have a single picture of each of Annie's parents, Andrew Murray and Amanda Allan-Murray. In his picture, Andrew is standing alone in a field, a tall, sturdy old man with a serious expression. My Aunt Doris took the picture of her grandfather back in the 1960s, with what had been her brand-new camera. From the unhappy look on his face, Doris took the photo against his will. Amanda's picture shows her young and dressed in a nurse's uniform. It was taken while she was working in Boston just after the turn of the century. I had no idea she had been a nurse before seeing this picture. She isn't smiling either, but that was how you posed for a photo back then.

One of the things that makes many Victorian-era photos interesting, and perhaps a bit unsettling, is the fact that no one is ever smiling. In the early days of photography it took a very long time to take a photograph, sometimes as long as fifteen minutes. This long exposure time was far too long for a person to hold a smile. A second reason is that people had really bad teeth, as dentistry was not yet a common practice. A person's smile would ruin an otherwise professional-looking picture. But the most widely believed reason was that people simply thought they looked silly when they smiled. If they were spending a lot of money on an important portrait, they wanted to look serious. This was the same reason you don't see people smiling in old painted portraits. To quote author Elizabeth Wallace, "A photograph is a most important document, and there is nothing more damning to go down to posterity than a silly, foolish smile caught and fixed forever."

American author Susan Sontag once wrote, "To take a photograph is to participate in another person's mortality, vulnerability, mutability. Precisely by slicing out this moment and freezing it, all photographs testify to time's relentless melt." We take pictures to preserve moments in our lives. To hold as keepsakes. To document our precious moments. We imagine pictures will be around forever.

When my paternal grandfather, Alex McKay, died in 2000, his death was unexpected. He had been lonely and depressed after my grandmother, his wife of more than fifty years, died of cancer in 1994. He didn't cope well without her. One day he fell at home and broke his hip. Although everyone assured him he would recover soon, he insisted he was going to die. It turned out he was right. He died at the rehab centre a few months later. His house was as he had left it.

My father urged me not to go back into the house. He said it was best to remember it as it had been: my second home growing up and the happy home of his childhood. He had no plans to go back inside. At the time, I agreed that he was probably right and didn't go. I regret that now.

My grandparents' home was a "the door's always open" kind of place. It was only a five-minute walk from our house, and I would visit almost daily as a kid. I loved being there when my grandfather would come home from work for lunch, which he did every day at 1:00 P.M. sharp, and everyone would gather in the kitchen.

I was in my twenties and living on my own in the city when he died. I was moving almost every year from one apartment to another. Physical keepsakes meant nothing to me then, and I didn't think to take anything of his or my grandmother's to remember them by. The enormous job of cleaning out their home—of sorting and dealing with a lifetime of belongings—fell to my uncle and his wife. They emptied out each room, plus the basement, with its countless storage boxes and antiques. When they were finished, a "For Sale" sign went up out front, and the house was gone from our family forever.

A few years later, I stopped into The V one afternoon to visit my father.

"You'll never guess what Jean-Paul found out at the dump," he said to me.

I had no idea who Jean-Paul was or why he was looking for stuff at the dump, but I followed Dad upstairs to the storage area above the service station to find out. There, propped up on the wall, was an eight-by-ten portrait of me and my brother as young teenagers. The picture, an unflattering representation of our awkward adolescence, had always been on display in my grandparents' family room. It was now water-stained and dirty. The frame was chipped and discoloured.

"Jean-Paul recognized Kevin and thought I might like to have it. Someone just threw it out in the trash!"

That someone had obviously been a family member who had been tasked with the cleanup at my grandparents' house. I didn't blame them for throwing it out. I would have done the same thing. That house had so much stuff, and none of us had room for any of it in our lives. Still, the idea of that picture at the dump bothered Dad. It remains on display in his storage area to this day. I couldn't help but think about the other photos from their mantel. What happened to all our old school pictures? And what about the group photo of the entire family together at my grandparents' fortieth wedding anniversary? Were they all rotting at the bottom of the landfill? Probably.

Modern society is leaving a very different photography footprint than generations before us. The cellphone camera, which was first invented in 2000, has made everyone a photographer. We take photos of everything these days. And we don't take just one picture, we take countless. At my daughter's junior high prom, I took more than two hundred pictures of her and her friends. When I was a teenager, we took one twenty-four–shot roll of 35 mm film at prom. Before digital, people were cautious with photos. Each print cost money when we picked them up a week or so later from the photo developer. But now, we can take as many as we want. Instead of physical albums, people store their images in online albums and on social media, and although people still make print copies on occasion, it's no longer common. The idea that these pictures will last forever still exists. But will they? When someone dies, their social media accounts could be deactivated or deleted. Even if they continue to exist, does anyone think to look at them? And is it strange if we do?

Mr. Fraser, the man who photographed the Murray quintuplets, went on to copyright his photos, and he sold prints, often in a small card format. One of the pictures I saw—the one belonging to Ernie Murray—was stamped on the back with "Jno. R. P. Fraser, Photographer, New Glasgow, N.S." (Jno. being an abbreviated form of John, I assume) in a fancy scroll. On the side it said "Negative Registered. Upper Stewiacke, N.S. MR 80." On the front it read in very tiny print up the left side: "Copyright Applied For."

The photographer died in November of that same year, 1880, at age fifty-five. A copy of his last will and testament is at the McCulloch House Museum and Genealogy Centre in New Glasgow. He left his archive of photos to his wife, who later left everything to their children. Neither of Mr. Fraser's children, Stanley or Sarah, had children of their own, and the photos were then left to a local photographer at Waldren's Studio in New Glasgow, who later sold them to the Dalhousie University Archives. Although the Waldren Studio Photography Collection—made up of more than 55,000 glass plate negatives, film, and prints, dating as far back as 1870—is now digitized and accessible, the original Murray quintuplets' photos and negatives are not part of the collection. No one seems to know what happened to them.

I don't know how many images were taken that day back in February 1880, but I've seen three different pictures of the Murray babies. There are two slightly different versions of the five together; the main difference is that the adult hand that is supporting little Jeanette on the left can be seen clearly in one and not the other. I've seen these photos in various old newspaper clippings and books. There is also a photo of just the four dead babies, which I found

The front and back of one of John R. P. Fraser's photographic prints of the Murray quintuplets. (Note, there is no adult hand visible in this version of the photo.)

on display at the McCulloch House Museum. It was of very poor quality, and not an original.

I desperately wanted to find the negatives just in case there had been a family photo taken. It's unlikely Adam Murray, being the old-time farmer that he was, would have wanted to pose for a photo, but maybe the photographer had talked him into it. Or perhaps there is a copy without the traditional Victorian-era oval frame that would allow us to see the person standing on the side holding the living baby. Was it Maria? One of the other children? A neighbour? My great-great-grandmother Elizabeth?

Back in the 1880s, Mr. Fraser's estate would have sold numerous copies of his famous pictures. A local barber shop in the town had a picture of the Murray quintuplets in the left-hand corner of its front window for decades. I heard about this from a descendant of the Murray quintuplets' family who contacted me after hearing I was researching the family story. Although she knew little else about the quints, she said this picture was the only photo she had ever seen of them. Other original copies of the picture are probably hiding in people's attics and old albums.

I was able to track down two original photos, and each had a story to go along with it.

My first encounter with Ernie Murray, the unofficial Murray family expert on the topic of the quintuplets, was that conversation we had in 2008 when I was a journalist at the *Daily News* in Halifax—and it hadn't ended well. When I started doing research for this book in 2018, I knew I would need to speak with Ernie again, but I was wary of phoning him for fear he'd shut down my questions again.

My Aunt Ginger and Uncle Fraser ran into Ernie one day at a community function. They started chatting and realized their shared connection to the Murray quintuplets. Ernie told Ginger where he thought the babies were buried. She told me later that he was talking quite openly and casually about it, and she was sure he'd be fine with talking to me again. Still, I was hesitant to make that call. When Fraser offered to do it for me, I was grateful.

I waited nervously in their living room while Fraser went into his office to phone. He came out a few minutes later smiling. "Ernie said he'd talk to you," he said and handed me an open copy of the local phone book with Ernie Murray's number underlined. "He said for you to give him a call Thursday afternoon to set up a time. You can meet him here at our house if you want?"

I thought that was a perfect idea. My aunt and uncle's home would be neutral ground.

A few weekends later I found myself back at their house, a beautiful, picturesque property they called Chapel Cove, overlooking the waters of Little Harbour. Ernie, a man in his seventies with white hair, a short white beard, and casual clothes, arrived promptly at 1:00 P.M. He was limping from an accident with his tractor but assured us he was on the mend. Under his arm was a large envelope with what I hoped was a treasure trove of Murray family history and secrets.

We sat down around the living room coffee table, and Ernie set down his big envelope in front of him. Everyone seemed a little uncomfortable and the conversation started awkwardly.

"I know I had some family history written down years ago, but when I went to grab it this morning, it wasn't where I thought it was," he told us, shaking his head in apology. "I looked everywhere. I'm afraid I don't have very much for you."

This was disappointing. Still, he had to know something. His great-grandfather was Adam Murray, making him a direct descendant of the quints' family.

Ginger told him the story we knew about how her great-grandmother Elizabeth went over to Adam and Maria's house by horse and sleigh and delivered the quintuplets. Ernie had never heard this story before, but he didn't dispute it. He couldn't. He didn't know anything about the birth.

"They never talked about it. Not ever," said Ernie with a casual shrug. "My mom died when I was fifteen, so if she had heard any family stories, I never heard them."

I noted that from what I was finding, it was typically the women who kept and shared the family stories, and the men were usually silent about subjects of birth and babies, especially *this* baby story.

"It was well-known within the family that the circus fellow P. T. Barnum approached them about buying the bodies," said Ernie. "I heard that many times throughout the years. They wanted to preserve them in wax, or something like that. That's all I was ever told about them. I was also told their house was the foundation you could see from the Egypt Road."

I explained that property was the foundation of our family's old farmhouse and that his ancestors had lived farther back from the road in an area that was now completely overgrown and hidden from sight.

Ginger went on to say that after her relatives died and their family farmhouse burned down, A. T. Logan, a former mayor of Trenton, bought and logged the land for many years. From there, the property changed hands numerous times, including a few years where Fraser and Ginger owned it for training Fraser's black Labrador retrievers. Fraser would take his prize-winning dogs to trials all over North America, and during that time, the land was well-maintained and free of small trees and brush. You could clearly see the foundation of our ancestors' old house and the adjacent apple orchard.

"There was a time when I actually wanted to sell our home here and build out there," said Ginger. "But we didn't. It was just such a beautiful place. We drove in once when they were building the homes that are there now, and the land just looked so different."

As the afternoon went on, the envelope Ernie brought with him remained unopened on the table in front of him.

"What did you bring?" I eventually asked him.

He picked it up and dumped out the contents: a few old newspaper clippings I hadn't seen before—and two photographs of the quintuplets.

I picked up the smaller of the two pictures and immediately noticed the stamp on the back. "Is this an original?" I asked.

"Yes. Someone found it in an old box of pictures, and it got passed along to me, because they knew I was a descendant." Ernie seemed pleased that he had brought something of significance for my story.

It was clearly old. The paper was cardstock, but soft. It was tattered on one side, as if kept in a wallet with only one edge exposed. It was a bit faded but still in good shape and much clearer than any of the newspaper photos I had seen. It may seem odd to say I was excited about an old picture, but I was. I was thrilled. I knew the photo I held in my hands had been directly purchased from the photographer, or his estate. It felt like a genuine connection.

Then Ernie handed me another picture. This was a five-by-seven glossy print of the same picture. "You can have this copy. I had copies made for some family members a few years back, and that's an extra."

The picture is blown up and printed in sepia tones, but it's still surprisingly clear and crisp for a photo taken more than 140 years ago. (This is the photo I now have framed in my home office. It's the version without the visible hand.)

We chatted for a while longer, and as he left I thanked him for taking the time to talk with me. He apologized again for not being much help and promised to keep looking for his missing family papers.

Although it was on the tip of my tongue, I never asked about the location of the grave. I was more concerned about keeping communication open. I would call him at a later time and ask. For that moment, I was happy to have the articles and the picture.

As for the second original photo, it would still be another year before I encountered it.

It's unlikely the photography session of the Murray quintuplets was something the family had arranged for themselves, given their desire for privacy. The photographer may have come on his own, or arrangements might have been made by a friend, a family member, or someone in town. Elsewhere in the world at that time, photographing a loved one in death was a perfectly normal thing to do.

I wondered about the origins of the once-popular, grim tradition. How did it get started? And why?

Sourcing books on the topic of death photography wasn't easy. I did a basic online search and then one on Goodreads. I was looking for the most highly rated books on the subject. I made a list of about five to check out. I then went to Indigo to find them. No luck. My next stop was Amazon. They had a few, but everything cost at least a few hundred dollars, even the used books.

My fifteen-year-old son and I were out running errands one day when I decided to drop into the local library and ask there. Armed with my list and library card, I went to the front desk. It wasn't until I started reading off the titles that I realized how strange my search sounded. I was requesting books with pictures of dead bodies. That was when my son decided to browse on the other side of the library as far away from me as possible.

"It's for a research project," I assured the librarian, who was probably wondering what kind of person would make such a request.

None of the books I was looking for were in the local database, but she explained how the interlibrary loan process worked. When I got home, I went online and filled out the form for each of the books on my list. It took weeks, but my search eventually turned up a few books that were transferred in from university libraries. One of them even had an old-style library card in the back. The most recent check-out date was seven years earlier.

Death photography, it would seem, is not a popular topic.

There's a scene in the 2001 haunted house movie *The Others* where Nicole Kidman's character, Grace, opens an ancient photo album only to find that everyone in it, young and old, is photographed with their eyes closed. They are in beds, sitting in chairs, holding hands, and lying in baby carriages. She shows the album to her housekeeper, Mrs. Mills. "Do you know what this album is? Look, they're all asleep." Mrs. Mills looks at the book. "They aren't asleep, ma'am," she says. "They're all dead. It's a book of the dead. They used to take photos of the dead in hopes that their souls would go on living through the portraits." Grace is horrified at the pictures, which is a natural reaction. It's not something anyone nowadays, or even in 1945—the year the movie was set in—would expect to see.

One of the early pioneers of photography was French inventor Joseph Nicephore Niepce. Niepce wasn't much of an artist, and he was trying to capture the likeness of a scene without having to actually draw it himself. Around 1826, he shot one of the first photos, looking out from an upstairs window, using a chemical technique called heliography. The image resembles a charcoal sketch and took about eight hours to expose. The idea caught on, and people have been steadily advancing photography techniques ever since.

The Victorian era—the years of Queen Victoria's reign from 1837 to 1901—was a particularly interesting time for photography, which was a new phenomenon. A new art. A new tool. The first effective form was called the daguerreotype. It was a small, highly detailed picture on polished silver. It was expensive, but less so than a painted portrait. By the mid-1800s, more photographers began to get into the trade, and it became more affordable and therefore more popular.

During this time, people—especially those in Victorian England—were obsessed with death. This wasn't surprising, given the diseases of the time. If cholera or diphtheria didn't kill you, then measles, consumption, scarlet fever, rubella, or typhus might.

It became common for photographers to take what they called a memento mori picture of a recently deceased person for the grieving family to have as a keepsake. The Latin words "*memento mori*" mean "remember you must die." The photo is an artistic and symbolic reminder of the inevitability of death.

Memento mori can take several forms and existed well before Victorian times. People might cut a lock of hair from their dearly departed and wear it in a ring or a locket, or make a wax death mask of a loved one's features. Images and symbols of death were common in paintings and sculptures. And then along came photography. Memento mori photography wasn't only popular in England—it became common all over the world. It was a source of pride and art for photographers and families. These pictures weren't kept hidden away in drawers and albums; they were displayed proudly on walls, mantels, and in other public areas of homes. People would even purchase, sometimes by the dozen, "black mourning cabinet cards" with a post-mortem photograph of the deceased to give to friends and family.

In the US, photographers regularly advertised their services for the bereaved. "We are prepared to take pictures of the deceased person on one hour's notice," one ad read. Although the studio was an option, the photographer usually made house calls. Photographers took the necessary props for staging with them, including black mats that were often decorated with floral patterns. Dead children were sometimes photographed with one of their toys, but most photos were not personalized.

Professional photographers discussed their work in trade journals. American photographer Albert Southworth, of Southworth & Hawes—an early photographic firm in Boston whose partners have been called "the first great American masters of photography"—described the process of photographing the dead in an 1873 panel discussion on techniques. "You can bend them till the joints are pliable, and make them assume a natural and easy position. If a person has died, and the friends are afraid that there will be liquid ejected from the mouth, you can carefully turn them over just as though they were under the operation of an emetic."

Although this is a morbid and candid description of a sensitive situation, it allows one to imagine what it might have been like posing the four Murray babies for their photos. Were they dressed when the photographer arrived? Or did he have to prepare them himself?

When embalming wasn't available, everything had to happen fairly quickly. The corpse would sometimes be laid out on a board of ice, and the viewing might even take place while the family waited for the coffin to be made. This was why some photographers advertised quick availability and services, as the entire burial process might be completed in a single day.

Sometimes a photographer captured only the person who had passed away, other times the entire family would gather for one last photo. Given the expense of the portrait, this was sometimes the only family photo they would have. Because of the long exposure time involved in taking a photo at that time, the dead would sometimes appear more in focus than the living people in group shots, as theirs was the only body that was fully still. It makes these photos even more unsettling.

Post-mortem photographers occasionally used an aid called a corpse stand, with which they propped the body up vertically; they then tied the body to the stand. The family members would gather around for the group picture. I came across one photo of five siblings, each half a head taller than the last. The caption below the picture said: "It was common for families to have lots of children, and also common for them to die before their fifth birthday. In this picture, the youngest child has died and is propped against a stand for the picture."

The dead were sometimes made to look as alive and lifelike as possible, which included posing them sitting up or perhaps lying down but with their eyes open. They might also be modelled to look as if they were sleeping. I came across a photo of a little girl surrounded by dolls. The girl was dead but arranged in a sitting position, as if she had simply fallen asleep while playing with her toys. There was another picture of twins, one dead and one alive. The dead one was surrounded by flowers. One photo showed a dead man posed with his two still-very-much-alive dogs. Some portraits would have an entire family surrounding a beloved dead child. Other photos would be staged similarly around a dead pet. Some photographers used what they called the "hidden mother" technique when dealing with babies — both alive and dead. The mother would be holding the child in her arms while hiding herself behind a sheet or blanket. A literal "veil" between the worlds. The hidden person is obvious, and the pictures have an eerie quality to them.

In contradiction, sometimes no special arrangements were made at all to make the deceased look lifelike. The family would prepare the body for the funeral by washing and dressing it, then tying their loved one's hands together so he or she would fit more easily into the coffin. Then the picture was taken.

I also came across pictures of couples; the live spouse posing with the dead, either both lying on a bed or one in a casket and the other at their side. Other mourning photos were of groups of people, often women, posing together in their elegant black bereavement attire, but with no deceased in the picture.

In some of the old photos I came across, the cause of death was evident, providing an extended look at life in those times. One picture was taken through an open window from outside a house, as the subject was a young man who had died of scarlet fever and the photographer wasn't able to go inside due to quarantine. Other photos showed children who were emaciated due to illness. Some had swollen necks, others had visible sores. The camera did not discriminate as it recorded the dead of the times.

Later in the Victorian period, photographers began altering photos. Sometimes this included adding pink cheeks and painting open eyes on a dead person's face.

Although early deaths and death photography remained common in the early twentieth century, by the 1920s, photographing the dead became more of a private, unspoken matter. Funeral homes became more common, where professionals looked after the dead rather than families, and with the convenience of film cameras, nurses in neonatal wards would often take photos of stillborn and preemie babies that were not expected to live, so families would have a tangible memory of the infant. To this day, there's an organization based in Colorado called the Now I Lay Me Down to Sleep Foundation that provides parents who have lost a baby with a free professional portrait. The organization asserts the photo provides an important step in healing for bereaved families. The foundation recruits and trains professional photographers all over the world, including Canada, and has provided more than forty thousand portrait sessions since 2005.

Even though we don't talk about it today, we still photograph our dead—young and old alike—fairly regularly. In the 1980s, 1990s, and early 2000s, funeral homes sometimes handed out disposable cameras in case people wanted photos. My mother kept a picture of her father in his casket in one of our family albums. People still have their memento mori, they just don't put them on display.

While I was researching this book, my Aunt Phyllis died. She had been living in a nursing home in New Glasgow, having lived the entirety of her adult life in a care facility. She passed away in her sleep in November 2018 from complications from pneumonia. She was eighty-two.

I hadn't been to visit her in well over a year. Although I didn't know she was as sick as she was, I had been thinking about her in the days leading up to her death. It had been way too long since my last visit, and I was trying to find a time to get in. I always had an excuse. Work, kids, life. I didn't think about her as much as I should have. When I did, I felt guilty. She was on my mind the day Ginger called to tell me she had passed away. I was too late for that visit.

The last time I saw her alive she was sitting in a wheelchair. Her legs refused to support her small, round body any longer. She sat hunched over. She was quiet, speaking only when spoken to. She wore her usual costume rings on each of her fingers and brightly coloured plastic necklaces around her neck.

My mother was with me that day. She pointed to me and said to Phyllis: "Do you know who this is?"

Phyllis stared at me a moment with her big, childlike blue eyes. "Anne," she said.

Ever since I was a little girl, she always thought I was my cousin Anne. Anne is twelve years older than I am and probably the last young person in the family Phyllis remembered. Her seizures and regular shock treatments had caused a great deal of brain damage, and as the years progressed, her memory didn't hold as it should. It was often stuck in the past.

"No, this is my daughter, Lori," my mother told her. "You remember Lori, don't you?"

Phyllis continued to stare at me, clearly not believing my mother. To her, I was Anne. In the early 2000s, Phyllis had lived in a group home near my house in Dartmouth. I would visit her sometimes, but unless my mother was with me, she wouldn't remember me from one time to the next.

Phyllis's funeral was a family-only event held at a funeral home in New Glasgow. My mother and I drove from the city for the afternoon service. The day was cold and rainy. We were the first people to arrive, and the funeral director took us into the room where my aunt was laid out. Ginger had selected a metallic pink coffin and had her sister dressed in a sparkly grey and black sweater, because Phyllis liked things that sparkled. I thought she looked peaceful, with the soft pale pink satin of the casket surrounding her face. She deserved a little peace after such a difficult life.

As we waited for the other family members to arrive, I snapped pictures of her in her casket with my phone. I don't know why. I wasn't going to post them anywhere or make prints. I just thought I should take one last photo.

There were about twenty-five people in attendance for the short service—her sisters and their families, as well as Phyllis's nieces, nephews, and cousins. The room felt empty with its many rows of unused chairs. The rain and bitter cold continued throughout the day, and everyone decided not to attend the burial at the cemetery that afternoon but to go the next day instead. After the service, the family went back to Aunt Ginger's for a late lunch.

Chatting with Ginger, I mentioned how nice I thought Phyllis had looked. I think this is something people often do when there's an open casket. They voice an opinion. The deceased either looked nice or they didn't. They either looked like themselves, or nothing like themselves at all.

"She did look nice, didn't she," Ginger agreed. "I wish I had taken a picture of her."

"I took one," I told her, pleased that I had thought to take a memento mori. I promptly texted it to her.

LITTLE EGYPT, 1880: AN UNEXPECTED TELEGRAM

News that the last Murray quintuplet had died travelled throughout town, but the death was only reported in the local newspapers. Most international papers never corrected the original stories that said the Murray babies were all doing well.

Still, the news had made it to one interested party in particular.

A telegram arrived at the New Glasgow telegraph office shortly after Jeanette's death. The office, which was more of a tiny booth, looked out across the East River to the bustling downtown of New Glasgow. The operator was likely excited when they saw the name of the telegram sender. The message was delivered swiftly to its destination: Adam Murray's farm in Little Egypt.

Adam and Maria did not receive many telegrams. Adam wasn't an educated man, but he could read and write. Still, it likely took him a moment to comprehend the intention of the message. The telegram was from American showman P. T. Barnum. The circus owner wanted to buy the bodies of the quintuplets for his show.

The message would also have indicated he wished to mummify them and take them on tour with the circus.

The Murrays were horrified. The shock they'd experienced during recent events was too much. First, the astonishing birth of five babies, followed by a flurry of attention and interest sparked by this seemingly impossible occurrence. Then there was the fear they felt regarding the daunting task of providing for five new mouths. Next came the sorrow and heartbreak as, one after another, the newborns died. The photo session that followed was also a numbing experience, as were the somber services and burials. And now, to add to their pain, this revolting offer: their precious babies reduced to a sideshow exhibit.

At that time, most people in Nova Scotia would have known the name P. T. Barnum. The famous man himself had been in the province just a few years earlier with his elaborate "Greatest Show on Earth." Frivolous entertainment such as a circus was not the sort of thing Adam Murray would have been interested in, nor did he have the finances to take his family and pay fifty cents for admission, a quarter for the children. Adam was a simple man and the family rarely ventured far from the farm.

But the dollar amount at the bottom of Barnum's telegram would have been more money than Adam had ever seen in all of his fifty-seven years. The family lived day to day and relied almost entirely on the land. They owned nothing of value.

Still, Adam and Maria were not interested. They may have sent a telegram back indicating as much, or perhaps their lack of reply was an adequate response.

As with the news of the births and deaths of the children, the townspeople soon got word of the American showman's offer. It was even mentioned in a local newspaper article that same week. Times were tough for many people in the county, and just because the Murrays were turning down the proposition didn't mean someone else wouldn't capitalize on the opportunity. Grave-robbing and looting was common at the time, but stealing actual bodies from a cemetery was rare. This was, of course, a special circumstance.

Under the cover of darkness, a handful of Murray men snuck back into the Riverside Cemetery to retrieve the recently buried caskets. The cemetery was designed for horse-and-buggy travel, and even with the snow, they were likely able to pull up close to the unmarked gravesite.

The ground was partially frozen, but the freshly toiled earth was loose enough that they could remove the caskets with relative ease. The men loaded the rosewood casket (or caskets) onto the back of the wagon and took them home to the Murray farm. They dug a shallow grave in the mud basement of the Murray farmhouse and interred them there, as any disturbance of earth on the property could also bring attention to a gravesite. Under the house, the bodies were protected. Hidden.

After that, life went on.

CHAPTER 11: EVERYONE LOVES A CURIOSITY

The bodies of the Murray quintuplets would have been a perfect addition to P. T. Barnum's circus sideshow. The babies were not only extremely rare and notable, but also something many people at that time would have thought impossible. Five babies at one birth? No way. Barnum was famous for making the impossible possible. A man with three legs. A woman over seven feet tall. A man with hair all over his body. Unbelievable? Not at Barnum's freak show.

The culture of the nineteenth century was one of curious minds. People looked for entertainment and for answers. It was a time of cultural and intellectual change. It was the century of Darwin's theory of evolution and also of literary legends such as Charles Dickens, Sir Arthur Conan Doyle, Mary Shelley, and Jane Austen. For the working class, it marked the emergence of dime museums—"lowbrow" galleries of curiosities—and "freak show" acts.

Today's public would never approve of such a show. But back then, these curiosities could not be explained by science. People who were different were simply strange, and a lack of scientific explanation made it somehow acceptable to stare and pay money to see them on display.

In 1880, P. T. Barnum was at the height of his stardom and was one of the most famous men, not only in North America, but in the world.

He travelled to all corners of the globe in search of his rarities. He visited Queen Victoria on multiple occasions. He had riches. He had fame. Everyone knew the name P. T. Barnum. But where Dr. Couney displayed babies on Coney Island for the purposes of saving lives and advancing science, Barnum showcased his "curiosities" for the purposes of fame and fortune.

Phineas Taylor Barnum was born in Bethel, Connecticut, in 1810. He came from humble beginnings. His father was an innkeeper, barkeep, and tailor. But Phineas had big plans for himself. In his twenties, young Barnum ran his own general store and opened a weekly newspaper. His editorials were often controversial, and he was sued for libel after writing stories against the elders of a few churches and was imprisoned for two months. The newspaper was a sacred piece of daily entertainment and society's main source for information.

At the age of twenty-five, Barnum moved to New York City where he started his first entertainment troupe. One of his first acts, Joice Heth, was also one of his most disputable. Heth was a formerly enslaved Black woman whom Barnum promoted and exhibited as the still-living 161-year-old nurse to George Washington. An 1835 advertisement claimed, "Joice Heth is unquestionably the most astonishing and interesting curiosity in the World!" People came to hear her tell stories, and they left not knowing what was true or not true. When she died a year later, Barnum set up a public autopsy and charged fifty cents admission. When the coroner said she was only about seventy-nine or eighty, Barnum claimed the corpse was not Heth, and that Heth was on a tour in Europe. Barnum once said, "As a general thing, I have not 'duped the world,' nor attempted to do so.... I have generally given people the worth of their money twice told."

In 1841, Barnum purchased Scudder's American Museum in New York City, which became the hugely successful Barnum's American Museum. At its peak in its early years, the museum had as many as fifteen thousand visitors a day. About 38 million customers visited the museum between 1841 and 1865. (It's interesting to note that the population of the United States in 1860 was under 32 million.)

Although he wasn't the first person to own and run a museum, he became known as the father of the "dime museum"—a nineteenth-century phenomenon dedicated to human curiosities—because he was the first to promote museums to the public in a way that not only made people excited but also truly curious.

From the beginning, the museum was a platform for Barnum to promote his human curiosities and also his hoaxes, the most famous being the Fiji (or Feejee) Mermaid. The mermaid was supposedly the mummified body of a real mermaid discovered in the South Pacific, where legends of the mythical creature existed. The mummified artifact was originally owned by a Boston sea captain who purchased it from Japanese sailors, or so the story went. The sea captain returned to Boston and died penniless. His son sold the mermaid to the owner of the Boston Museum, who leased it to Barnum. It was exhibited at P. T. Barnum's American Museum in New York in 1842, where it quickly became one of his most popular attractions. At some point over the years, it disappeared and was believed to have been destroyed in one of the museum's fires. The Peabody Museum of Archaeology & Ethnology at Harvard

University says its "Feejee Mermaid" in the museum's All the World is Here show is actually Barnum's. Other institutions also make this claim. Barnum was said to have created multiple replicas of the mermaid, so it's possible other originals do exist.

Hoax or no hoax, Fiji mermaids remain of interest to the general public today and are still on display in museums and attractions all over the world. I stumbled upon one at the Ripley's Aquarium of Canada in Toronto. My first thought was that the artifact was Barnum's original—it really did look that real—but I quickly realized it must be a replica. I can see why the mid-nineteenth-century museum goer would question it. The information below the Toronto mermaid explained that it was once exhibited as a genuine mermaid. Thousands of people paid twenty-five cents to see Barnum's Fiji Mermaid in 1842. Barnum insisted his mermaid was the real thing until, in his old age, he admitted it was "just an ingenious fusing of the upper half of a monkey and the lower half of a fish!"

Barnum's human curiosities were not all hoaxes, per se, and were thought by the general public to be truly wondrous.

One of his side-show favourites was Myrtle Corbin, The Four-Legged Woman. Corbin had a little-understood condition called dipygus, which caused her to have two separate pelvises side by side from the waist down—but Barnum's audiences didn't know that. Then there was Frank Lentini, The Three-Legged Man. Lentini's third leg and small fourth foot (as well as, apparently, a second set of "reportedly fully functioning" genitals) were actually those of a conjoined twin. Longtime Barnum attraction William

Henry Johnson, also known as Zip the Pinhead, was at the centre of Barnum's "What Is It?" attraction for more than forty years. The question Barnum posed was, "Is it a man or an animal?" Johnson wore a fur suit and was displayed in a cage where he yelled and shrieked at guests. It is believed that Johnson had a condition known as microcephaly, which caused him to have an oddly shaped head and small stature.

One of the most famous "freaks" of the nineteenth century was Joseph Merrick, known as The Elephant Man. Not associated with Barnum's shows, Merrick became a household name after the 1980 movie *The Elephant Man* was made about his life. Merrick was born in 1862 with unidentified genetic defects that caused his skin and bones to be covered with growths and tumors. The tumors were thought to have been caused by his mother being frightened by an elephant while she was pregnant, hence the name "Elephant Man." He was a novelty exhibit in the back of a shop on Whitechapel Road, London, for many years and later went on the road with a travelling fair.

People have always looked for explanation of the unexplained. In 1880, people didn't understand how five babies at one birth could be possible. It was, in fact, the rare occurrence of an unusual egg and sperm combination. It wasn't magic or something the mother did that caused it to happen; it was natural, and could be explained by science. But before the unexplained was understood, it was wildly misunderstood—and for audiences of the day, there was a certain amount of pleasure in outrageous speculation.

The dime museum and freak-show acts served not only as a popular form of entertainment but were also a valued source of employment for the performers, who might otherwise struggle to find work. A job with Barnum, or a similar show elsewhere in the country, offered up a life with people who shared equally strange characteristics. Barnum's star acts were paid generously. He brought them both fame and fortune.

Charles Stratton, General Tom Thumb, was one of Barnum's most famous attractions. Stratton joined Barnum when he was just four years old. Barnum taught the boy, who was under two feet tall, to dance, sing, and entertain, and told the public he was eleven. Stratton became a star and an eventual partner of Barnum's. When Stratton died at age forty-six, he was a millionaire with a wife, a mansion, a yacht, and horses.

Two of Barnum's famous curiosities actually hailed from Nova Scotia—both giants with Scottish roots and East Coast charm that made them perfect for the stage.

Angus MacAskill of Cape Breton was seven feet, nine inches tall and weighed 425 pounds. His shoulders measured forty-four inches, and his shoes were nineteen inches long. The palm of his hand was nearly a foot wide. He was considered handsome, with deep-set blue eyes, a husky voice, and a pleasant manner. He could carry barrels weighing more than three hundred pounds under each arm, hoist a ship's anchor weighing more than two thousand pounds, and even lift a full-grown horse over a four-foot fence.

The 1981 *Guinness Book of World Records* called MacAskill the "largest true giant" to have ever lived. His stature was proportional in every way—his size and strength were natural genetic gifts, and he showed no signs of the typical characteristics of a "pituitary giant," which would have attributed his excessive growth to over-activity of the pituitary gland at the base of the brain.

Born on the Isle of Berneray, Sound of Harris, Scotland, Angus and his family were forced to leave their land in the 1830s during the Highland Clearances. Like the Murrays, the MacAskills travelled from Scotland to Nova Scotia for a new life. They settled in Englishtown on St. Anns Bay, Cape Breton, where young Angus—who was an average-sized child at the time—began to grow. And just kept growing.

In 1849, MacAskill joined Barnum's circus and performed alongside Barnum's famed General Tom Thumb. Queen Victoria heard of MacAskill's strength and invited him to visit Windsor Castle in 1853. She called him "the tallest, stoutest, and strongest man to ever enter the palace." She gave him two gold rings to show her appreciation.

MacAskill retired wealthy and young and opened a general store in Cape Breton. He died unexpectedly of a brain fever in 1863 at age thirty-seven. The giant's grave in Englishtown's Auld Cemetery is a popular summer tourist attraction. The grave was forgotten for a time until someone brought new interest to the story in the mid-1900s, which led to the restoration of the gravesite.

In 1862, Barnum sent an agent to New Annan, Nova Scotia, to inquire about twenty-two-year-old Anna Swan, who was seven feet eleven inches tall. Barnum offered her a thousand dollars a month to be a "giantess" on exhibit at his American Museum in New York. She took the offer. She became "Miss Anna Swan, The Nova Scotia Giantess —The Largest Woman in the World." Barnum touted her as being eight feet one inch tall, and she was often on display beside Commodore George Washington Morrison Nutt, who was only twenty-nine inches tall and twenty-four pounds.

Anna's parents and siblings were average in stature, so her size was not attributed to genetics; a likely tumour on her pituitary gland, located at the base of the brain, caused an overproduction of human growth hormone. Anna was four feet tall by the time she was five and was sometimes referred to as the "infant giantess."

Part of the appeal for Anna to work for Barnum was the access to education that he offered her. She studied music and had a private tutor. According to Anna's great-great-nephew Dale Swan, a volunteer at the Anna Swan Museum in Tatamagouche, NS, Anna was known to be a person who could handle Barnum. She often stood up for herself and sometimes refused his proclamations and requests.

Through the circus, Anna met Martin Van Buren Bates, the "Kentucky Giant," who was seven feet nine inches tall. The pair married in 1871, and Anna wore a dress that was a gift from Queen Victoria. When Anna and Martin went back on tour, they were advertised as "The Tallest Couple in the World."

Anna and Martin desperately wanted children. She became pregnant in 1875, but sadly the baby, a daughter who weighed eighteen pounds, died in childbirth. Six years later, Anna became pregnant again. This child, a boy, weighed twenty-three pounds and twelve ounces, and measured thirty inches in length. Unfortunately, he died just hours after birth. Anna and Martin's son is still the largest known human birth on record.

Anna died of heart failure at the couple's home in Seville, Ohio, in 1888. She was forty-one years old. Her heartbroken husband sold their oversized home and ordered a statue of her from Europe for her grave in Seville. A museum in Tatamagouche, NS, is dedicated to her life story.

Barnum's American Museum was destroyed by fire twice, first in 1865 and then again in 1868. The devastation of the second fire was so complete, Barnum decided to retire from the museum business altogether. He had many endeavours throughout the years. He promoted the famous Swedish opera singer Jenny Lind on her American tour. He started hospitals, aquariums, and wax museums, and for a time he entered politics. He was mayor of Bridgeport, Connecticut, and also a member of the Connecticut House of Representatives. But in the end, what he loved most was entertaining curious onlookers and making money while doing so.

In 1870, when Barnum was in his sixties, he decided to get into the circus business. His first circus was "P. T. Barnum's Grand Traveling Museum, Menagerie, Caravan & Hippodrome," which he coined a travelling circus, menagerie, and museum of "freaks." It was later called "P. T. Barnum's Travelling World's Fair, Great Roman Hippodrome, and Greatest Show on Earth." He always used his name, which drew attention, and usually an assortment of "greats." Who could resist going to "The Greatest Show on Earth"?

The merging of Barnum's curiosities with the glam of the circus offered the public something new. He had transported the museum to the circus and created the "side show," a performance idea that would be continued and taken to new levels on New York City's Coney Island, which opened its popular "freak show" in 1880.

The year 1880—the year of the quintuplets' birth—was an important year for Barnum. Although his fame brought people into the seats of his circus tent, his wasn't the only show in town. The Cooper and Bailey Circus was Barnum's main competitor, and Barnum sought to merge the two. That summer, Barnum and James A. Bailey signed a contract to create what would later be called the Barnum & Bailey Circus.

Barnum visited Nova Scotia for the first time with his 1876 "Greatest Show on Earth" travelling world's fair. As the trains rolled into Halifax on August 1 that year, it was a sight to behold. Three monster trains hauled 120 railroad cars full of performers—acrobats and trapeze artists, trained elephants, curiosities, and artifacts "from every Clime," and a "Noah-like menagerie!"

According to newspaper articles of the time, the turnout and excitement for the 1876 show in Halifax was impressive, with about nine thousand tickets sold in the middle of a summer heatwave. The trip was particularly memorable for the city because, as the circus paraded through the streets, the staff at the Bank of Nova Scotia on Hollis Street went out to watch, and thieves made off with about $22,000. As documented in Dean Jobb's 1990 book *Crime Wave*, the culprits were never caught.

The circus was often followed by unsavoury people. "Thieves hang around Barnum," the local paper editorialized on August 5, 1876. The day before the show came to Halifax, they performed in Truro, a town about an hour north, and the train station was robbed while the circus performed.

The show and the bank robbery were the talk of the city for years. At least one local hotel, Halifax's Waverly Inn, boasted for decades that Barnum was once a guest there. It was still a boutique hotel in the city's beautiful South End until its closure in the early 2020s. At the time of Barnum's visit, its location was considered on the "good side of town," away from the trains and the dirt and industry.

The 1876 show was part of a North American tour with more than one hundred stops, including six in Canada, all of which were in New Brunswick and Nova Scotia. Most years, the circus stuck to a route in the United States, keeping an audience Barnum understood and catered to. But he would sometimes vary the route, likely to keep attendance numbers high, as new viewers meant more ticket sales. Numbers at shows had been dwindling at some US stops. In 1873 and 1877, the tour included a few stops in Ontario. In

1879, of the more than a hundred towns and cities the circus visited, sixteen were in Canada, including one in New Glasgow.-

The true age of the Coney Island sideshow came in the early 1900s, with Lilliputia, a miniature city inhabited by so-called "midgets and dwarfs," and Dreamland, which promoted all sorts of "oddities," many of whom were former Barnum stars. The shows stopped in the mid-twentieth century when they fell out of popularity with the general public. The change can, in part, be attributed to a transformation in people's attitude toward these shows. It was no longer acceptable to stare at people who had physical differences, and audiences felt the shows exploited those people. Many of the performers, however, didn't feel exploited. When the shows shut down, they were left without work and a way of life many had enjoyed.

The Coney Island Circus Sideshow still exists today, on a much smaller scale. Modern sideshows focus on people who created their own freakish acts, such as people who eat fire, charm giant snakes, swallow swords, or cover themselves in elaborate tattoos.

To confirm the story of Barnum's financial offer to the Murray family, I contacted the Barnum Museum in Bridgeport, Connecticut, to see if they had any official records. Unfortunately, they had no relevant documents from this time period and couldn't confirm or deny the claim. They also couldn't estimate how much the offer might have been, although they did say it was likely substantial.

The only proof I could find were two newspaper clippings. A 1971 *New Glasgow Evening News* article titled "Canada's First Quintuplets" included an interview with Dan Murray, Adam and Maria's grandson, and read, "It was reported later that Mr. and Mrs. Murray had been offered a large sum of cash by P. T. Barnum, who wanted to mummify the bodies and put them on exhibition." And a February 1880 article in the *Colonial Standard* from Pictou, Nova Scotia, that said, "It is currently presorted that a Yankee showman offered the parents a large sum of money for the bodies of the infants."

It was assumed that showman was Barnum, and the story went from there.

LITTLE EGYPT, 1880: LIFE WENT ON

The days lengthened, and winter passed. Spring arrived, which was typically a joyous time on the Murray farm. The children could once again play outside and get out from under their mother's feet. The lifeless fields began to turn green, and blossoms started to bud on the russet apple tree outside the little farmhouse.

The quintuplets were rarely mentioned after the funeral, even among family members. It was in the past. Yet, for a time, the bodies were still buried in the basement of their home. Three months later, when the story became old news, and the ground began to soften, the family knew they would have to find a new resting place for their children.

Adam and Maria found a spot in the woods near their home. It was, perhaps, a spot near a cluster of tall trees—trees that cast some shade from the burning afternoon sun. It was a place no one would recognize, remember, or find. It might even be near where the family buried the three children they lost in 1875, little Elizabeth, Margaret, and George.

Once again, under the cover of night, the Murrays moved the small caskets. They took them from their shallow basement grave to this special spot in the woods. They didn't make a big deal of it—they didn't even particularly discuss it. Only a handful of family members were ever shown the location, and everyone who was shown the spot was sworn to secrecy.

Adam and Maria went on to have another five children; they had eighteen in total, ten who survived. As the children grew, they all eventually moved away to homes and families of their own. Adam passed away in 1908 and was buried in an unmarked grave in the Little Harbour Pioneer Cemetery. There was no money for a headstone, and the exact location of the grave is unknown. Maria, twenty-five years her husband's junior, started a new life. What shape that new life took, however, is lost to history. She may have worked for a time at a local store. She might also have become a midwife herself. One rumour claimed she got married again and moved to Halifax.

None of the Murray children were interested in working the farm, and after Adam's passing, the animals were sold off, the fields became overgrown with trees, and the barns were left to rot and collapse. A distant relative known only as Mona—she of the rubber boots—moved into the little farmhouse. With the fields no longer tended, a narrow path through the woods was the only indication the house existed at all. For years, that road was known as Mona's Lane. Eventually, the house was deserted and left to vandals and the elements. And the people of Little Egypt no longer remembered the house was even there.

CHAPTER 12:
NOT FORGOTTEN

When I first started researching this book in the spring of 2018, people were not talking about the Murray quintuplets of Little Egypt Road. It was when I started asking around—contacting various Murray family members and inquiring at local museums and libraries—that the story came to light again. At my request, people were evoking old memories, searching their attics for newspaper clippings, and looking through old books and archives.

The Pictou County genealogy enthusiast who had helped me research my family tree was chatting with a local councillor one day and mentioned he thought there should be a memorial of some sort to commemorate the story of the quintuplets. It is a significant piece of local history that people don't know about, he told the councillor. The councillor agreed. The idea of a plaque for the Murray quintuplets was put forth to council and approved. A date, time, and location were set for a plaque unveiling, and the Murray family was invited to attend.

It was only by luck that while doing some research online I came across a public service announcement in a local paper about this event, which was to take place on a Saturday afternoon in early February 2019 (which would also mark the 139th anniversary of their birth). I was surprised and disappointed that not one of the family members or historians I had talked to contacted me to let me know this was taking place. I had initiated the research, after all. I had also left my name, contact info, and business card all over town and could be easily reached. Perhaps they didn't think I was serious about the book? I wondered if they thought of me as an outsider. Here I was, a woman whose last name wasn't Murray, digging up a story that had long been considered a family secret. And although I had grown up in Pictou County, I no longer lived there.

I felt disheartened, but still wanted to attend.

My mother and Aunt Doris agreed to go with me. Mom and I drove up from the city that morning and picked up Doris in New Glasgow. When we arrived at her house I asked if I could pop in to see the Murray heirloom mirror that she had told me about in one of our previous conversations. She had explained that it once hung in the farmhouse parlour and was the only artifact she had from the old family homestead. Mom and Doris were in a hurry—they both hate being late for anything—so I was given the green light but for a quick peek only. The mirror was smaller than I expected and at a glance it seemed almost ordinary, like something you'd find in a modern furniture store. Yet, taking a closer look, I could see its age in the darkened corners of the glass, and the unique designs in its ornate hand-carved frame. I snapped a photo with my phone, cherishing it as a tangible link to the farm. Even small relics like this mirror held special meaning for me. I was on a mission to find every detail about the family during that time. The mirror, a witness to countless Murrays over the years, might have even reflected the faces of the quintuplets' parents and siblings at some point. Secretly, I wanted to take it home with me.

The plaque unveiling for the Murray quintuplets was to take place at the municipal building in Pictou, where the plaque would eventually hang on the wall in the first-floor gallery hallway. I always pictured a monument for the quintuplets at a local cemetery or ideally on the Murray property, but that wasn't practical given that unrelated families now resided on that land. I also imagined I would be the one responsible for its existence. But circumstances had taken it all out of my hands.

Because my mother is perpetually early for everything, we were the first arrivals at the municipal building parking lot. I insisted we wait in the car for others to arrive. Vehicles eventually began pulling in, and as people got out of their cars, Mom and Doris immediately started recognizing faces. "Oh look, that's 'so-and-so' Murray from Trenton," and, "You remember him...'so-and-so' Murray's brother." As it turned out, between the two of them, they knew most of the fifty-plus people in attendance.

The actual ceremony was in the council chamber room, and the chairs filled up fast. Murray descendants were invited to put on a purple ribbon to signify their connection. We knew we were not "descendants" and didn't take one, but as we discovered later, a lot of the people who wore the purple ribbons were not actually descendants either. Like us, they were distant relations, and most had no idea how, or even if, they were actually connected. Some simply had the last name Murray. I wished they had said "relatives" instead of "descendants" so we would have felt included.

The event attracted local politicians as well. A few addressed the crowd and spoke about the importance of history. Two local historians also said a few words, including Clyde Macdonald, whom

I had spoken to previously for my story and who had himself written a book about Pictou County history that included a chapter on the quintuplets.

In his short speech, Macdonald touched on the part Dr. William Fraser played in the birth, noting that although it was common in the 1880s for women to have their babies delivered by a midwife, the Murray family had one of the best physicians in the area. There was no mention of my great-great-grandmother and her role in the delivery.

Doris, who was sitting beside me, whispered rather loudly, "It was Grandma who delivered those babies, not the doctor."

Then they unveiled a small plaque. It had no headline and contained just a few paragraphs, including the doctor's name, when and where the babies were born, the weight and length of each baby, how long they lived, and the fact that four were buried together and the fifth alongside the others. It also noted that Mrs. Murray had three children after the quintuplets for a total of fifteen children. (According to my research, Mrs. Murray gave birth to five children after the quintuplets for a total of eighteen; ten surviving and eight lost).

Although I'm glad something exists to commemorate the quintuplets, as there had been nothing for 139 years, I was disappointed in the content and design of the plaque itself. Once more, the historical record is not complete, and the contributions of women had been omitted.

All said, the "ceremony" lasted about thirty-five minutes.

Someone took a group photo of the family descendants—which included those who were probably not descendants at all—and then everyone moved out to the foyer for a small reception. There were sandwiches, cookies, tea, and coffee, but I never saw them, as I didn't actually make it to the reception area tables.

I don't typically enjoy networking, but this event was a perfect opportunity for sourcing information, so I began introducing myself to people and telling them about my book. Most were interested in not only hearing about my research, but also in telling me what they knew. At one point there was a small line of people waiting to talk to me.

"I never saw the house," one man said, "but I remember the road to get into it. We used to call it Mona's Lane." I told him I had heard stories about this "Mona" but never heard it called Mona's Lane before.

"Did you know about the blinds?" one woman asked.

"Yes," I said. The curtains—as my grandmother called them—had always been her favourite detail of this story. The curtains (or blinds) were never reported on in any of the articles or stories written about the quintuplets. It's one of the few stories that was 100 percent handed down through the generations. "But please tell me what you heard."

"They didn't have enough blankets and had to wrap some of the babies in the blinds from the windows. They were green blinds with little tassels."

I had imagined the curtains to be green but had no way to confirm if my grandmother had told me this detail or if I had simply imagined them that colour. I was thankful for this family member's validation. If she had heard this same detail, it was likely to be true.

In the crowd of Murray relatives that day was a childhood friend of mine named Karen Murray. I hadn't seen Karen in decades. We were friends when we were eight. I remember the age because we played with our new Cabbage Patch Kids together; the dolls were at the height of popularity in 1983. Karen's family moved away before we hit junior high, and I never saw her again.

When I was a child, my grandmother told me Karen was a direct descendent of one of the quintuplets' siblings. Armed with this exciting information, eight-year-old me mentioned this connection to Karen on one of our Saturday afternoon playdates, but she had no idea what I was talking about. I told her all about the five babies born out in Little Egypt, but she showed little interest. If anything, she looked at me like I was weird. I never brought it up again. But I remember being jealous. Karen had a true link to the family, and could not have cared less, whereas I had only tidbits of the story and was thoroughly obsessed.

Karen and I chatted briefly at the plaque dedication ceremony. She offered to ask her relatives if they had any stories and contact me if she found out anything. I wondered whether she remembered that conversation about the quints those thirty-plus years before as clearly as I did. Or at all.

I also spoke with a local reporter who promised to mention my quest for information and include my email address in his article. In the days and weeks following the event, I received a few messages from family members.

One person living in the US found the story online and reached out to me via email:

> *Dear Lori, I have been sorting through old memorabilia of my grandmother's and found a photo and typewritten 'death notice' of the Murray quintuplets' birth. I remember my grandma telling me at one point that we were distantly related (Rankin was the family name and I believe the maiden name of the mother). I just googled the birth and found a Pictou story with your contact information. I'd be happy to mail you these items if they would be of help to you.*
>
> *All the best, Heidi*
> *Maynard, Massachusetts–USA*
> *great-great-great-granddaughter of Jean Rankin*
> *born June 15, 1819, Barneys River, Pictou NS*
> *died June 13, 1883, Pictou Landing, Pictou NS*

I wrote back with an enthusiastic yes! I couldn't wait to see what she had to send.

A few weeks later, a couriered package arrived. Inside was a handwritten note: "Hi Lori, Here is the typewritten notice and photo that I found in my grandmother's keepsakes (her name was Claretta Marshall Pehrson). Good luck with your book, it's an amazing story. Nowadays those babies would have all survived!"

The death notice was nice to have, as it was full of details and typed on thin, old paper, and had clearly been well preserved. The info was all stuff I'd seen before. It was the picture she sent that practically brought me to tears.

I am likely the one person in the world who would be excited to get this old, slightly morbid photo in the mail. (I was even more excited when I realized it was a different photo than the one Ernie Murray had. This picture had the adult hand in it, just like the newspaper article picture. And the babies were propped up a little more, so you could see their faces more clearly.)

I now consider it one of my most cherished possessions and I take it out of the protected envelope I keep it in every once in a while and just stare at it, wondering what was happening in the room around those babies in that exact moment.

I was one of the last people to leave the municipal building the day of the plaque dedication. Doris had a sore knee, and she and Mom went out to the car to wait for me. When I finally made it outside, someone was locking the doors behind me.

My cheeks hurt from smiling and my mind raced with ideas. I had been desperate for family information, and this opportunity to talk with Murray relatives about my book was a gift. I wanted to keep chatting about it with Mom and Doris, but I sensed they had heard enough on the subject for one day. My questions to them about my grandmother and the Murray farm had been relentless in recent months.

We went for a late lunch at a little café Doris liked in downtown Pictou, and we chatted casually about my kids, Doris's son Murray, the weather. Because my mother and Doris had never been particularly close when I was growing up, I had never gone out for lunch—or dinner, or even coffee—with just the two of them before. It was nice. I hoped this visit was the first of many to come, but I worried that instigating future meals together would still be left to me. Would I make the effort without my book project to propel me? I knew I was interested in my family's past, but what would it take for me to be as committed to my family's present and future?

I don't remember the last time I saw my grandmother. It was probably a few weeks before she died. Although my days were busy then—Molly was two and a half and Max was just nine months old—I would visit and call regularly. A visit with Grammie wasn't a chore. She was close with all her grandchildren.

Our visits were typically short—just as they had been when I was a kid. She wanted to hear what was happening in my life, and I would fill her in. She would hold the baby and fuss over my toddler, and then she'd say she was tired. She'd turn her cheek, poised for a goodbye kiss.

My grandmother's last home was the Shiretown Nursing Home in Pictou. She had sold her tiny home in Trenton a few years before, deciding that after being alone for more than thirty-five years, she no longer liked the solitude. It likely had something to do with the fact that she didn't feel confident enough to drive anymore and had lost the freedom and independence her car had allowed her.

For a short time, she lived with my mother. My parents were divorced by this time, and my mother, looking for a distraction, wanted to help. She had recently moved into a new house and renovated a "granny suite" for Grammie. No one in the family thought the arrangement would work, and it didn't. The two women were too different, and Grammie soon put her name on a nursing home wait list.

The Shiretown Nursing Home offered the best of both worlds for a senior like my grandmother: companionship and nursing care, but also some independence and solitude. Grammie had her own private apartment and joined the other residents for lunch and supper, which were served in a cozy dining room. But she complained about life there as well. The place was full of old people and none of them interested her.

In the months before her death, she told me on more than one occasion that she was ready to die. She was still healthy, but her body ached. Most of her sisters had already passed away and the others were housebound. She had buried two husbands. All arrangements had been made for her and Phyllis's funerals, as well as for Phyllis's continued care. She was ready.

When my mother called to tell me Grammie had passed away, I wasn't entirely surprised, but I was still devastated. My grandmother may have been ready to go, but I wasn't ready to lose her. We never are when it's someone we love. In accordance with her wishes, there was no autopsy. Although the doctors noted there was a wad of gum in her throat—she always loved her spearmint gum—they couldn't confirm that she'd choked. They didn't know what had caused her death. She simply went to sleep and never woke up.

I wrote a short eulogy, which I read as we said our final goodbyes at Heatherdale Memorial Gardens. The speech included a list of my top ten Grammie B traits:

10) her mayflowers;

9) her gingerbread with lemon sauce (the only thing I ever remember her baking);

8) her car (which she cherished and loved buying new every year);

7) her beep (when she would visit us and we'd go out to her car for a short visit);

6) her gum and peppermints (she always had some in her big purse);

5) her generosity;

4) her truthfulness;

3) her love of Javex bleach;

2) her independence;

1) her family.

One of my cousins later reminded me that I missed one memory: her early bedtime routine. I couldn't believe I'd forgetten how she'd put us to bed at 6:30 P.M. when we stayed at her house for a sleepover. It was, perhaps, a habit she picked up during her many years living on the Murray farm: "early to bed, early to rise" was the way of life on the farm.

Collectively, my brother, cousins, and I all shared similar memories of her. It's interesting how certain characteristics of people stay with us. One small thing will evoke memories, trigger recollections. Grammie was undeniably unique and memorable because of her many quirky traits. I can't help but wonder what I will be remembered for.

I didn't keep a diary as a kid (unless you count the "diary" I used to diligently record what I wore to school each day—because, you know, those are important historical facts!), but I did have shoeboxes filled with mementos. Silly things like napkins from restaurants we visited on family vacations, a piece of my old bedroom wallpaper, the bathroom flooring before it was replaced, pictures and letters from friends and old boyfriends. They were all properly dated for reference and stored away on the top shelf of my bedroom closet. I was a family archivist, a keeper of our stories, even then. And yet, as the years went by, I forgot those mementoes were there.

After my parents' divorce in 2000, my brother bought our family home. He lives there now with his family. A few years ago, my sister-in-law came across my memory boxes in a storage area in the basement of the house. My mother must have put them there after I'd moved out. My sister-in-law brought them to my place, and we went through the contents together. I told her the story behind each item. We laughed about some, but most of the old keepsakes made me feel sad. It brought me back to my time in their house when it was my home. The boxes chronicled the years from when I was about eight to eighteen, from childhood through to young adulthood. I missed the family of four we were back then. I missed the home my mother made. I thought of the friends I don't see as often as I'd like anymore. Smell is a trigger of memory, but these things—these insignificant treasures of old pictures, notes, and random items from a past life—had an even stronger effect. The memories were vivid and clear.

While working on this book about the quintuplets, I constantly wondered about the Murray family. I wished desperately that I could peer into a memory box of their life on the farm. What kind of people were they? What did they look like? What did they like to eat? What did they wear? Unfortunately, I know so little about them that even making educated guesses seems impossible. In my imagination, they remain a silent and mysterious family with undefined faces, their tragic story of death being the sole detail I truly know about them.

The few local newspaper articles written about the family at the time described Mrs. Murray as "a strong, healthy woman." There was little else. They didn't even bother getting her actual age, referring to her as "a little more than thirty years of age." Most of my research shows she was thirty-three. They described Mr. Murray as "an ordinary sample of physical development—in fact, he is below the average in stature and bodily proportions."

One article from the *Boston Post*, February 20, 1880, took the description a bit further:

> *'About four miles from New Glasgow,' says a correspondent of the* Chronicle, *'there is a settlement called Egypt, a cold, stony, half barren place. There dwells Adam Murray, rather a sickly specimen of the hardy Highland race from which he sprang. His wife, on the other hand, is a strong, healthy, rugged woman, of about thirty-seven years of age.'*

Surely if Adam had a friendly and outgoing way about him, he would have been described in a more agreeable manner. Does this tell us something about him? The reporters who wrote these stories were clearly including someone's opinion of the pair. Perhaps they asked a neighbour or community member who knew of them and that's all this person had to say. This same general description of the couple was repeated countless times in articles over the years. I'm still using it today.

I have a copy of Adam and Maria's marriage certificate, which states they could both read and write. Yet there were never any written journals or albums that I know of, except for the family Bible. Bibles and other religious books were used for recording family births and sometimes deaths as records to be passed down through the generations. Aunt Doris has her grandparents' hymn book from our Murray farm. Her great-grandmother Elizabeth Murray penned the names and birthdates of each of her children on the inside cover in a neat black script. It's an important keepsake to have, as it is the only memento that exists for many nineteenth century families when they're gone. Though I've never seen Adam and Maria's Bible, I saw a note on Geneology.com that a family member somewhere in Ontario has it, with the names inside. I would love to someday catch a glimpse of it, or at least see a photo of the family page. It would confirm the names and birthdates of the family members and offer me a chance to see the handwriting. Was it Maria's hand that scripted the names? Or Adam's? Or another family member altogether? Was the cursive neat or child-like? It would serve as another resource—of which there are precious few—to bring me a step closer to the story.

It's worth noting that same *Boston Post* article (February 20, 1880) also said, "No doubt Mrs. Murray will receive Her Majesty's usual gratuity in such cases, or rather, usual in cases of triplets, for cases of five children at a birth are not common." There is no record of the Murrays receiving any correspondence from Her Majesty Queen Victoria, who was known at that time to show an interest in the lives of her subjects by reaching out when significant events occurred. It's unlikely she did contact the Murrays, given that the children all died soon after birth, and that the family did not seek fame or fortune.

I knew most of my grandmother's six blue-eyed, blond-haired sisters—some better than others. They all married, except for Elizabeth, and most had children.They were a memorable group of women; all were as beautiful in their senior years as they had been when they were young, with their fair hair and clear, pale skin. Some had strong personalities, and they used to bicker amongst themselves on a regular basis.

While researching this book, my grandmother's sister Elizabeth's name came up again and again. She was named after her grandmother, the midwife of the quintuplets' story, and was considered the family caregiver. She looked after her aunts and uncles on the farm and then later her parents in their old age. There's a famous quote by Pulitzer Prize–winning historian Laurel Thatcher Ulrich: "Well-behaved women seldom make history." Although I believe this quote has truth to it, I also know there are women who led selfless, silent lives who deserve to be remembered as well. When I think of this, I think of Aunt Liz.

I knew her as a kindly old woman. My mother and I visited her at the nursing home when I was a kid. She smiled and chatted pleasantly with us, stealing glances at the soap opera playing on the tiny television attached to her wall. The other women who shared her room quietly did the same. When we left the nursing home, Mom and I always talked about how sweet she was. I remember my mother saying she was grateful her aunt never made her feel guilty for not stopping by more often.

In her twenties, Liz was often on the Murray farm lending a hand. She was the only one of her eight siblings who never married. Because she had no family obligations of her own, she ended up doing the cleaning and cooking for her bachelor uncles. I wondered whether this was by choice. It's hard to say. Maybe she enjoyed it, maybe she didn't. No one seems to remember—had anyone ever asked her? When her father, Andrew Murray, passed away in 1953, the job of looking after her disabled mother also fell to Liz. She cared for her mother and stayed in her family home in Trenton until her mother died in 1965.

Having a family member dedicated to looking after the elders in a household is something that happened frequently in past centuries. There was often a "spinster" or "old maid," as they called them, left with this responsibility. When I asked my aunts Doris and Ginger what they remembered about Aunt Liz, they both said, "Oh, she looked after Grandma." That had been her role in life.

After her mother (my great-grandmother Amanda Murray) died, Elizabeth lived in the house for a few years. Her sister Ethel moved in for a time after her husband passed away, but then she got an apartment on her own. Elizabeth was lonely. She suffered a small stroke in her mid-fifties, and with no one to look after her, she moved into a nursing home. Within weeks, someone burned her family home to the ground. Like my grandmother's little guest house and the old family farmhouse in Little Egypt, which were both destroyed by arson years earlier, the guilty person or persons was never found. It may seem like three house burnings is beyond tragic for one family to endure, but the relatives who told me the stories told it in a matter-of-fact way. Back then, if you left a house vacant in the Trenton area, someone would burn it down. There was no modern security equipment available to help keep an eye on things when you weren't around.

There was no insurance on the house in Trenton and Liz ended up living in that nursing home until her death in 2001—more than thirty-five years. She'd walked into a nursing home a relatively young woman and never left. Aside from the one stroke, her health was always good.

Memory can play tricks on us. When I asked my mother why Aunt Liz moved into the nursing home, she told me it was because Grandma had died and she couldn't afford the house. When I asked her cousin Jeanie the same question, Jeanie thought Liz moved into the nursing home because she was lonely. It was Doris who remembered the stroke. None of them remembered many details about Liz's life. Doris recalled that Liz loved music and could sing and chord on the organ. And that she was always kind. "I remember for my thirteenth birthday she made me a big cake with pink and white icing, and we ate it out on the farm," she said.

When I asked my mother why Elizabeth never married, she said, "I think she may have been hurt badly by a past love."

One day my mother and I were going through some old newspaper clippings, and we came across Liz's obituary.

"She died in 2001?" my mother said in surprise. "Why wasn't she at your wedding?"

I was married in 2000. My grandmother was there, as were some of her sisters. But not Elizabeth. Had she been ill? Or did we all just forget to invite her?

"Did you not go to her funeral?" I asked.

"I must have. But I don't remember," my mother said.

Doris did. "Of course I remember," she said. "I sat with her when she died." Her words brought a sense of solace to me. After my mother's reaction to her obituary, I imagined Elizabeth completely alone and forgotten.

Some part of me worries about being forgotten myself. I wonder what kind of mark I will make on this world (aside from the legacy of my children, of course). This fear is one of the reasons I write. Books and articles are things people keep around, at least for a time. My name could exist forever on the stories I've written. I also think about the role other people's published works played in keeping the quintuplets' tale in circulation. Without their articles and books, many of the story's intricate details would have faded into obscurity. Author Susan Orlean wrote about her own fear of being forgotten in *The Library Book*: "Writing a book, just like building a library, is an act of sheer defiance. It is a declaration that you believe in the persistence of memory." My husband, Jeff, paints watercolours as a hobby and shares my view on the subject. "I like the idea that my art will be around even when I'm not," he once told me.

When it comes to the people in our lives, we always remember those closest to us, but others can slip from our memories. We might think of them when we come across an unexpected reminder—a picture, a gift, a holiday—but not necessarily every day. And when the people who knew us are gone, we are no longer remembered at all. We become a name on a headstone, an obituary, a face in a photograph.

CHAPTER 13: FINAL GRAVES

When I was in eighth grade, we were given a social studies assignment to visit a local cemetery and make chalk gravestone rubbings of old headstones. My mother suggested the cemetery across the road from our family church in Little Harbour. It was an obvious location because not only was it ancient, but it had a family connection.

My mother parked in the empty church parking lot, which is only used on Sunday mornings, and we quickly crossed to the other side of the road. The church is located on a bend, and cars often take the turn too fast. At the entrance to the graveyard is an old-fashioned-style sign that reads Little Harbour Pioneer Cemetery Est. 1852; behind it is an overgrown path leading into the woods. There's a bit of a bank off to the left, and as a kid I used to look there sometimes to check for coffins coming out of the ground. Someone told me that happened sometimes with old gravesites. There's an old cemetery near our cottage just a few kilometres up the coast where, rumour has it, after years of erosion the caskets were seen sticking out of the cliff for a time before eventually falling into the sea, leaving only the headstones.

I remember walking up the path to the Pioneer Cemetery, which I found incredibly spooky, then sitting on the wet grass with my craft paper and black chalk and making a record of some of the people buried there. I concentrated on the oldest burial dates I could find, which went as far back as the mid-nineteenth century. I'm sure my mother told me at the time that some of them were my ancestors, but the names held no significance to me then.

There's a photograph of thirteen-year-old me in the cemetery that day. I'm wearing a yellow sweatshirt with the hood up. I'm standing between some old headstones with my craft supplies in a plastic grocery bag around my wrist. I appear bored, but I don't remember feeling that way. This was around the same time I started reading Stephen King and V. C. Andrews. I loved books and movies that terrified me.

Graveyards loomed large in pop culture at the time. Michael Jackson's "Thriller" video was still topping the charts and I watched it hundreds of times. To me, the cemetery, with its weathered gravestones standing like silent guardians, was a place where you could almost hear the whispered tales of ghosts from bygone eras. What ancient family secrets would they share if they could? Following that cemetery visit with my mother, I developed an interest in graveyards that never went away. To me, it was a realm where time stood still.

When my family goes on road trips around the province now, I sometimes make my husband pull over so I can take a quick walk around an old country graveyard and snap a picture or two. Every small town in the province has a collection of old churches and graveyards that document the area's past. I like to search out the oldest headstone. My husband and kids typically wait in the car, amused but rarely interested enough to come along with me. I see old cemeteries as places of mystery and unknown stories. Many people—like the rest of my family, for example—don't seem to notice them at all. They drive by without a second glance.

My search for Murray graves brought me back to the Pioneer Cemetery in the summer of 2018. Carol Stewart, a Murray family descendant I'd met at the quintuplets' plaque unveiling, told me she believed Adam and Maria were both buried there.

Decades before, Carol's great-aunt Edna Murray White (granddaughter of Adam and Maria) took Carol on a tour around Chance Harbour and Little Harbour to show her the family gravestones. Their search included a drive to the Little Harbour Church, which actually has two graveyards: the Pioneer Cemetery and the newer, larger, sprawling Church Brook Cemetery behind the church.

Edna, who was born in 1910, referred to both of these graveyards as the Stewart Mills Cemetery. That was, apparently, what her generation had called it. The Stewart family once owned a gristmill up the road near where the local store is now. Back then, people would name a place after a family who lived nearby. These informal names would usually stick, but in this case it was forgotten. The gristmill closed at some point and the family moved away. Today, no one knows the cemetery by its original name. Aunt Ginger, who has lived a five-minute walk from that cemetery for more than sixty years, had never heard it.

Edna's parents, George Murray (Maria and Adam's son, sibling to the quintuplets) and his wife, Isabella, were buried in the newer section of the cemetery. Carol and Edna visited their grave that day, but the older Pioneer Cemetery wasn't accessible at that time.

"The cemetery across the road was just woods," Carol told me. "Someone was just starting to cut the trees to clean up the cemetery then. We never entered because Aunt Edna said there was no stone anyway."

Even though I had already heard there was no headstone for Adam, and likely not for Maria as well, I wanted to take a look for myself. Maybe I would find some secret marker that indicated a hidden grave in the surrounding woods.

After a lazy day at the beach, I asked my daughter, Molly, and my niece, Casey, if they wanted to go check it out with me. I promised mystery, intrigue, and the spookiest cemetery they'd ever seen. They agreed, more because they were bored than curious.

The cemetery and church are about a fifteen-minute drive from our cottage. This is the church I spent all my Sunday mornings in as a child and teenager, and where my husband and I were married back in 2000. I hadn't been inside in years. My daughter had not been there since her brother was baptized there in 2005, and she had no memory of that day.

Just as we pulled into the empty parking lot, a mist of rain covered my windshield.

Molly looked up at the threatening sky, her eyes narrowed. "I think I'll just wait in the car."

Nova Scotia weather is unpredictable. A sprinkle of rain could be a sign of a downpour to come, but it could also mean sunny skies within the hour.

"Let's just take a quick look around," I said. "Come on. It'll be fun."

The girls put on their jackets and reluctantly agreed to go with me.

The sky was filled with grey clouds as we walked up the little path, and the cemetery appeared even darker than I remembered it. The girls were successfully spooked. The rain stayed light, which didn't help scare off the mosquitos—the attacks came swift and fierce—and I knew our visit would be brief.

The Pioneer Cemetery is surrounded by tall trees, keeping it in almost constant shadow. With very little direct sunlight reaching the ground, the freshly cut grass was littered with brown patches and broken tree branches. There are about thirty headstones arranged in no particular order. Some have several names on them. One interesting family plot had a rusted iron fence surrounding a single lonely headstone, with the rest of the family's designated space remaining apparently unused.

I knew there were Murrays buried there, and this time the names on the headstones meant something to me. One stone read: *John Murray 1833–1905 and his wife Elizabeth 1845–1921* (my great-great-grandparents); *James Murray 1875–1959* (Uncle Jim). On the adjacent stone marker: *Elizabeth Rogers 1873–1962* (Aunt Libby) and *Sarah Murray* (her sister) *1884–1968*. These were the people from the farm—the characters in the story I was trying to recreate.

I started to tell the girls all about them.

"Elizabeth was the midwife who delivered the quintuplets," I said excitedly, pointing to the names. "And this is Uncle Jim, Nana's favourite great-uncle. He used to drive around in an old Model T Ford long after modern cars were common. And these names here, Libby and Sarah, they were the last of the Murrays to live on the farm."

Molly and Casey listened patiently to me rattle on as they swatted at the insects that were eating them alive. Casey, at least, seemed interested, but I knew the girls couldn't appreciate these people the way I did. To them, they were just names that would soon be forgotten. There wasn't an old farmhouse to show them to help explain the family's way of life; there weren't even pictures of most of these long-lost ancestors.

Although we found other Murray headstones, those were the only names I recognized. There was nothing indicating Adam and Maria were buried there. We searched the woods beyond the headstones, looking for any sign of an unmarked grave. There were indeed sunken areas where graves might have been, but nothing definitive. The ground was too uneven and overgrown to tell. I felt frustrated. To me, a cemetery was a place for remembering and documenting our past. Yet standing there I was left with even more questions. If someone had taken the time to transport a body to the graveyard, dig a grave—which would have been, no doubt, a labourious task—and bury them, you would think they would have left some sort of marker. Was it a rock that eventually got moved? Did someone draw a map and mark the spot with an X? Did they note the body was fifty feet from the road and twenty to the left, for example? If so, where was that information? Lost to time?

I later checked with the church to see if there were any old records of unmarked plots, but I was told there were none. They did, however, confirm the likelihood of unmarked graves. This meant it was entirely possible, even likely, that at least Adam was buried there. If Maria had indeed remarried after Adam's death, she was probably buried elsewhere.

Another theory is that Adam was buried in Little Egypt, somewhere in the woods behind the old farm property, alongside the eight young children he and Maria had lost.

We'll never know for sure.

The word *cemetery* is Greek for "sleeping place." The use of a common burial ground for humans dates back thousands and thousands of years. The difference between a "graveyard" and a "cemetery" is that a cemetery is typically larger; a graveyard is usually associated with a church. I use the terms interchangeably, as no one locally seems to follow this rule.

One of the oldest gravesites in the world is thought to be Taforalt in Morocco, a cave burial that dates back more than fifteen thousand years. The world's largest cemetery, Wadi-al-Salaam in Iraq, is 1,485.5 acres and contains more than six million bodies. Most towns and cities in the world have burial grounds for their dead. The majority are public, but some are on private land. Others are completely hidden and unknown. Very old burial grounds are often rediscovered during construction or archaeological investigations.

Graveyards and death have always invited superstition. Some people believe you should hold your breath when you pass a cemetery to prevent inhaling a restless spirit, or that you should place coins on the eyes of the dead so they can pay the boatman in Hades to take them to the afterlife. In fact, at the Chicago Historical Museum, you can actually see the coins that once weighed down Abraham Lincoln's eyes. And did you know most cemeteries have headstones facing east? This is so when the dead rise up, they will face the sun, and possibly a new world. You're also supposed to remove a corpse from a house with his/her feet first, ensuring they won't look back and signal the people behind them to follow. (This is still typically done, but mostly because it's just easier to move a body that way.)

There is a certain etiquette expected when visiting a cemetery. There's the obvious—be respectful and quiet, don't touch the monuments/headstones, and never leave any trash about. Fake flowers and walking on burial plots—instead of between headstones—are also commonly frowned upon.

I remember one summer when I didn't follow proper cemetery decorum.

After our high school graduation in 1993, my friends and I scattered all across the province and beyond for university. But each year we'd all come home to spend our summers in Pictou County. Many of us still do. I remember one summer in my early twenties when one of our favourite party spots was a place we called Deadman's. After the bar closed on a Saturday night, we would somehow make it back to a friend's cottage where we'd walk along a private beach to a secret path that led to a hidden graveyard high up on a hill. There, we'd hang out amongst the old headstones, party, and tell stories until we were so scared we'd take off running to the safety of the moonlit beach.

Given the respect I have for cemeteries today, I realize this was discourteous and probably not the best idea. Still, I remember it as harmless fun. We may have left a beer can or two lying about, but we did no real damage.

This cemetery doesn't have a sign advertising its name, which is probably why people always call it Deadman's. An online search told me its official name is the Chance Harbour Donald Cameron Cemetery. There are many graves there—far more than the little Pioneer Cemetery—but there is no public access. You can only get there via a long walk from a nearby beach or through private land. "No Trespassing" signs are common on properties along the roads. The friend whose cottage we partied at once upon a time no longer stays there, and I've since tried to revisit the cemetery and had no luck finding a place to park.

Chance Harbour Donald Cameron Cemetery was another stop for Carol Stewart when she was out looking for family graves with her great-aunt Edna. Carol said they stopped at R. B. Cameron's house in Chance Harbour during their search in 1996—Cameron was a well-known Pictou County businessman who died in 2000—and his private nurse gave them permission to cross the land and offered directions to get there. It had been more than sixty years since her great-aunt had seen her grandparents' headstones.

"It's very secluded," Carol pointed out. "We drove over hayfields and down a long grassy road through the woods to get there."

Because I couldn't figure out a way to get back to the cemetery, I searched online and found a website that had pictures of many of the headstones. Most were local Scottish family names—Fraser, MacGregor, and Cameron. Although I didn't see any Murrays, there are undoubtedly related family members buried there, including Edna's grandparents.

I find it curious that I could visit this cemetery virtually but not walk among the gravestones myself. Many of the seniors who remember those buried there would not be computer savvy enough to navigate such a website. Nor would they choose to. It's yet another way we are forgetting our ancestors. If a cemetery is meant for remembering, why are more actions not taken to make sure they are accessible? The province is littered with forgotten graveyards; at least this one is remembered, even if it's not easily visited.

As I mentioned, on the day of Aunt Phyllis's burial in November 2018, we didn't go to the cemetery following her funeral service. The weather that day offered up a mix of snow and rain and below-freezing temperatures—typical stay-inside November weather. There was a family plan to visit the cemetery the next day, but as far as I know, no one went that following day or any of the days after for a service.

It was nine months before I made it there to pay my respects.

It wasn't a planned trip. After a weekend at our cottage, I was on my way home to Halifax alone one afternoon when I stopped to pick up a coffee at the highway gas station for the almost-two-hour drive ahead. The idea struck me, and I decided right there and then to visit the cemetery. I knew it was nearby, but it had been so long since I'd been there, I couldn't remember exactly where it was. A quick online search told me I was just eight minutes away.

The last time I'd been to the Heatherdale Memorial Gardens was for my grandmother's burial in 2005, fourteen years before. When I thought about how much time had passed, I felt guilty. The purpose of a cemetery and marker is for family to have a place to go. I even liked cemeteries; still, it hadn't been enough to propel me to visit. It doesn't mean I don't think of her often. In addition to having Grammie's picture up in my home office, I have some of her furniture in my house. Her antique wardrobe, for example, is in our bedroom, and I love that when I open the door, it still smells exactly like her bleach-clean house.

Heatherdale is one of those park-like cemeteries with flat grave markers. A few benches, a smattering of trees, and life-size stone statues of Jesus in various positions of prayer jut up from the otherwise clear, rolling hills.

As I drove in, I passed a sign that read: "We kindly ask that only fresh flowers be put on graves." When I looked across the perfectly manicured lawn, I noticed ornamental vases and fresh flowers everywhere. People did visit. Just not me.

It was late in the afternoon and sunny. There was no one else there, yet it didn't feel eerie or deserted. It felt like a public space, and I was simply lucky enough to have it to myself.

As soon as I stepped out of my car, blackflies swarmed my head. Biting insects seemed to be a common theme for my cemetery visits. I opened my trunk and changed from my flip-flops into a pair of sneakers. I held my keys in my hand and was about to lock the car—I'm a habitual door locker—but it felt wrong. There was not a living soul in sight. The beep would be an unnecessary disturbance in this peaceful place.

As I started across the lawn, my sneakers were immediately caked in mud. The ground was soft pretty much everywhere, with no high-ground dry spots to walk on. I found myself jumping from flat grave marker to flat grave marker (even though I knew this was against cemetery etiquette). As I neared the spot where I thought Phyllis's grave might be, I started looking for new grass. Phyllis had been buried in the winter just nine months before. I expected the grass to still be sparse. Then, I spotted it. But instead of new grass, it was a large mound of mud. It hadn't even been seeded yet. Did someone have to call the cemetery people to make that happen? Was that the family's responsibility? I had no idea. Still, I worried we, the family, had been neglectful. Had everyone forgotten about her as I had?

I made my way over and stood on the grave marker, which had no vase of fresh flowers, and looked down at the names. Annie Margaret Brown (née Murray), 1916–2005, Mother. Beside her on the same stone was Phyllis Anne Brooks, 1936–2018, Daughter.

I wondered which was worse: an unmarked grave that nobody knew about or a marked grave that nobody visited.

Out of curiosity I looked to see who had the neighbouring grave. I didn't expect it to be someone I knew, but it was. It was my best friend's mother in-law. On her grave was a vase of fresh flowers. When I asked my friend about it later, she told me her father in-law visited the cemetery often. It made me consider the different ways people grieve and remember. As I stood amidst the low-profile Heatherdale gravestones, a gentle breeze carried the scent of the fresh flowers, and a flood of memories washed over me. I might not visit often, but I was there. People visit cemeteries for many personal reasons—from grieving and healing to contemplation and reflection to maintenance and research—I was there to pay my respects and to remember.

Other loved ones were also in Heatherdale, including my grandfather, Fred Brown, though he was not buried beside Grammie.

Although I had only been to his grave once as a child, I remembered it was under a tree near the road. It took me a good half hour, but I eventually found it. If I had to pick a spot where I would like to be buried in that cemetery, it would be right there. It's secluded and well shaded under a beautiful old tree.

I only had a handful of memories of him, yet I felt just as emotional standing at his grave as I had at my grandmother's. Maybe it was because he was there all alone, or perhaps it was because I knew more family history now. I thought of the stories my mother told me about how my grandfather would stay out on the Murray farm and help Uncle Jim when he and my grandmother weren't getting along. The farm had been a refuge for him, just as it had been for my grandmother when she needed it—and for generations of Murrays, I now knew.

Later, when I told my mother I visited the cemetery and stopped by her father's grave, she told me she had never been to it. This meant it was my grandmother who had taken me there as a child and not her. Grammie must have cared for him at least a little.

"Why didn't you ever visit?" I asked her. I wasn't judging; I was genuinely curious.

"I don't feel a person's presence at a graveyard," she said. "To me, it doesn't feel like there's anybody there."

I never did ask Ernie Murray where he thought the Murray quintuplets' final grave was located; I didn't have to. He had already told Ginger when they ran into each other at that local community event and started talking.

"He didn't say it was a secret," she told me. "He was talking quite openly about it."

She said Ernie thought they were buried in the Riverside Cemetery. She also told me exactly where. But I still didn't know how he came to that conclusion, so I called him and asked.

I expected his story to be about a family secret passed down through the generations. A tale from his grandfather to his father to him. His answer surprised me.

"It was a next-door neighbour [to the farm] who told me," Ernie said. "His name was Lincoln Cameron. He contacted me about fifteen years ago and told me he thought I should know where they were buried."

Lincoln was getting up in years, and he wasn't sure if anyone other than himself knew the exact location. He told Ernie he was sworn to secrecy by the Murray family (exactly who told him isn't known) and had kept the secret as long as he could. Lincoln, who has since passed away, took Ernie to the cemetery to show him the precise location of the unmarked grave.

"I was always told they were buried on the farm," I said to Ernie on the phone.

"I always thought that, too."

"What do you think now?"

"I would go 99 percent that it's the cemetery," he said. It made sense to Ernie that this farm neighbour knew the truth. Ernie's older relatives never talked about the quintuplets, so it wasn't a surprise to him that they never told him or his siblings the location.

For me, this theory brought even more questions. If the quintuplets were buried in the cemetery as their final resting place, was the rest of the original story false—all that business about the family moving them from the cemetery to the basement, and finally to an unmarked grave in the woods? Perhaps they had never left the cemetery in the first place and the story was just a ruse.

"Do you think they were ever buried under the farmhouse?" I asked.

"I think so. I remember years ago I heard them [his family] talking that they were buried in the basement for a period of time. It might have been only a few days, until the excitement died down.

"I went out to the old Murray farm property only once," Ernie told me. "Seymour Calhoun was lumbering there at the time. I saw him there cutting trees, so I stopped in. He got interested in it, too.

We searched those woods for the graves, but there was nothing there. Nothing to find."

The Riverside Cemetery is located along the bank of the East River in New Glasgow along the Trenton Road. It dates back to the mid-1800s, maybe earlier, making it one of the oldest cemeteries in the county. It's the final resting place of many prominent townspeople, including businesspeople and politicians. Some have significant monuments. The cemetery has hundreds of headstones, most with several family names engraved on them. It is also known for having unmarked graves within its perimeters. It's believed to have as many as 120 "butterbox babies"—infants who died in childbirth or shortly after birth, born to unwed mothers; the babies' bodies were quietly buried in butterboxes.

Another local legend suggests there was once a pirate treasure buried there. In 1876, neighbours claimed they saw a group of people in the southwest corner of the cemetery digging under a large spruce tree. The treasure, thought to be hidden there by early French settlers, was then supposedly dragged down to the East River and carried away by boat.

Treasure or no treasure, that cemetery is the keeper of many long-forgotten secrets and stories. Unfortunately, many of Riverside's oldest tales have been lost. A plot-by-plot map of the cemetery, which likely also tracked even the unmarked graves, was among the documents lost when the New Glasgow Westminster Presbyterian Church burned down in 2011.

Other historic cemeteries in the area, such as Duff Cemetery near Stellarton, had records. A detailed list of unmarked burials at that cemetery includes 349 names, along with dates and ages. More than 180 of those names were children who died young or at birth. Similar numbers could be assumed at the Riverside Cemetery—but once again, the information I sought was lost to fire and time.

I drove to Riverside a few days after my conversation with Ernie. I wanted to see "the spot" for myself. Although I knew the grave—if indeed it existed—was unmarked, I still hoped to find some hidden clue. Some indicator they were there.

Riverside Cemetery is like many old cemeteries, where the buildings just seemed to grow up around it. The entrance is located directly off a busy main street. I arrived late in the afternoon on a weekday; if rush hour traffic existed in the small town of New Glasgow, I had hit it. There is no road into the cemetery; as soon as you pull off the main street, you're there.

The directions I had to the unmarked burial spot were clear. I parked and walked to it easily. It's an open space where perhaps a headstone could stand. There was no telltale sunken casket indentation in the earth or large rock acting as a marker. There was nothing there but green grass.

The noise of cars driving by was distracting. I decided to walk farther into the cemetery. I noticed that names on some of the older headstones had worn away almost completely due to age, neglect, and the elements. Other headstones had fallen over and lay broken. It's the responsibility of the families to look after the headstones, but as I've realized through researching past generations—and through my own experience—we forget about the dead.

I took my time walking around and then circled back to the spot. I stood there for another moment and tried to imagine what the cemetery might have looked like 140 years earlier. There would have been far fewer headstones. Were any of the same trees there then? Probably not. The nearby busy street would have been unpaved and used only by horse and buggy. No noisy traffic. The view across the East River would have changed drastically as well, as the other side was now littered with new homes.

I squinted my eyes and tried to see Adam, Maria, and their older children on that cold February day. Did they stand in this exact spot with their old, worn hand-me-down coats and boots? I imagined a flock of birds in a clear sky, a solemn goodbye.

I left without a sense of closure. I had no idea whether the babies were buried there or not.

One year, when Aunt Doris was young, she went out in search of a Christmas tree with her Uncle Jim. It was a family tradition for them to find a tree on the farm for her grandparents' living room, where she was living. Once chosen and cut, they would load the tree onto the sleigh and Jim would drive it into Trenton.

"We were in the woods out behind the Murray farm and Uncle Jim stopped walking and pointed toward a grove of trees," she told me. "He said, 'That's where the Murray quintuplets are buried.'"

She said it wasn't a particularly memorable spot, describing it as "just a place."

"Do you remember where you were? Any general idea?" I asked.

"I couldn't say now. But the story has always been that they were buried somewhere on the farm. Uncle Jim grew up on that land. He lived there most of his life. He would know."

I remember a conversation I had with my grandmother about the quintuplets when I was about twelve. She was cleaning mayflowers in her kitchen sink, and I was sitting at her little two-seater table. There were small pale-pink bouquets lined up in front of me in water glasses, or as she called them, "tumblers." The best way to describe the scent of mayflowers would be sweet and perfume-like, and just the right amount of both.

I had gone out with her and Teenie for the afternoon on their search. I'm not sure exactly where we went that day. It was some dirt road off the highway. She parked her Toyota Tercel in a field near a sparsely wooded area. The ground was uneven, and she and Teenie—two big ladies nearing seventy, wearing cotton knee-length dresses, black pumps, and head scarves to protect their hair-sprayed curls—got out with their plastic bags and started picking.

I didn't have a bag of my own and followed them around until their backs became too sore to bend down; then I would do the flower-picking and they would hold the bags open. When every last flower was picked, we loaded them into Grammie's trunk and headed back to Trenton. Grammie dropped Teenie off at her house before heading home, which was just a three-minute drive away.

I never asked how they knew where to find the mayflowers. It's a mystery. I haven't seen a single mayflower since my grandmother died.

As she washed the mud off the flower roots that day, we talked about the quintuplets' grave, which was something we often did when it was just the two of us. I was perpetually curious. I needed to know: Were they buried in a cemetery or out on the farm? My grandmother didn't even know which local cemetery it might have been.

“I don’t understand why they would have moved the caskets back to the cemetery,” I said. “It doesn’t make sense. They must still be at the farm. Maybe they were never at the cemetery at all.”

“Oh, they were definitely at the cemetery at some point,” she said, certain.

“So they were at the cemetery, then buried in the basement of their home, then in the woods, and then in the cemetery again?” It didn’t seem plausible to me.

“I’m not sure,” she said. “But I know for certain they were buried in the cemetery at one point and in the basement at another time.”

“And then elsewhere on the farm property?”

“Yes,” she said. “In the end, they were buried somewhere in those woods behind the farm.”

Like the location of Adam Murray’s grave, we will probably never know where the quintuplets were buried. But that was always what the family wanted anyway. They wanted them hidden, safe, and left alone in their final resting place.

CHAPTER 14: SEARCHING FOR MAYFLOWERS

I wanted to visit the old Murray farm property one last time. I didn't expect to find the graves, but I still believed it was possible to find the foundation of Adam and Maria's home. It was there in those woods somewhere—of that, I was sure. I wanted to stand in the spot where their home once stood. Where the babies were born, and where they died.

I printed out aerial shots from Google Maps, and I had a plan of where I wanted to search. There were areas I hadn't explored when I'd walked the land before. I didn't know any of the families who currently lived on or near the land and would need to get permission to look around. I asked my husband's Uncle Bruce if he'd come along with me again, as he had when I'd visited back in 2008. I thought we could park at his brother's place and walk through the woods again. What was once considered the Murray Farm Settlement was hundreds of acres of land, with at least two or three hundred acres between the two original farm properties. From what I could tell, Adam and Maria's house had been somewhere in the woods north of Bruce's brother's place.

In one of the aerial photos I had looked at, I noticed a break in the trees that may have been what people once called Mona's Lane. We could theoretically reach this potential "lane" from either of the properties. In an ideal situation, I would find the path, follow it along, and at the end we would find an obvious depression in the ground: the foundation of Adam Murray's farmhouse. And just maybe there would even be a russet apple tree beside it, as Doris had seen when she was a child. Even in winter, when the branches were bare, I could distinguish the unique shape of an apple tree from all the other trees that naturally populated the area.

We set out on a Sunday morning in early May. The day was grey and cold. The spring of 2019 had been fairly miserable up until that point, with lots of rain and only rare glimpses of the sun. I wore a turtleneck, long pants, a raincoat, high wool socks, and rubber boots, covering as much skin as I could to protect from blackflies and ticks. I finished the ensemble with a generous spray of bug repellent.

Bruce's brother's place wasn't visible from the road, so it wasn't until we came to the top of a long driveway and the road branched into two that the houses come into view. Bruce hadn't actually called to arrange anything with his brother as planned, so no one was expecting us. The morning was eerily dark and quiet. His brother's neighbours' place was the house I'd visited eleven years before. It looked different that day. The back woods were not as accessible as they had been. There were fences, garages, and new roads.

"Why don't we just drive in the main driveway of the other Murray farm and knock on one of those doors?" Bruce suggested, and I agreed. I hadn't set foot on what was once my great-great-grandparents' property since I had been there with my grandmother almost forty years earlier. In addition to finding Adam and Maria Murray's old home foundation, I wanted to see the foundation of my ancestors' home as well as the spot where my grandmother's little guest house once stood.

But I was instantly anxious. I hated the idea of knocking on strangers' doors for permission to walk their land. In response to my apprehension, Bruce said, "The worst they can do is say no."

There were two homes on the land then; both were set back at the top of the properties, far from one another and far from the road, but still visible.

We tried the farthest home first. There were two vehicles in the driveway, so it looked like someone was home. But when we knocked and rang the doorbell, no one answered. After a few minutes, we left and drove to the other house.

This home was large and beautiful and positioned to offer what I thought was probably the best view of the property. As I walked up to the door, the same anxiety nagged at me. Dogs began to bark inside; if people had been sleeping, they were asleep no longer.

After a minute or so, a woman opened the door. A dog ran circles around us on the doorstep. I explained to her that my grandmother used to live on the property—that was the simplest, quickest explanation—and asked if I could walk around in search of the foundation of the old house. The woman told me it was her son's house, and everyone else was still sleeping. She suggested we come another time. Maybe later that day. I took down their number and apologized if I woke her, which I knew I had. I was disappointed, but I had a phone number of someone to talk to, so that was a plus. Still, I was there, and the land was just waiting all around us.

As we walked away, she yelled out, "I think there was once an old barn there by that flagpole." She pointed. "They found a lot of stones in that location when they were building the house. You can still see them. Take a look."

The flagpole was in the front yard near the driveway, so we walked over. Flat stones were easily visible in amongst the new spring grass. They looked like randomly placed steppingstones. As I stood there, I looked over toward the overgrown grove of trees where I knew my great-great-grandparents' home once stood. The proximity worked. The flagpole was exactly where our old Murray barn would have been.

My mother has a picture of her on the farm when she was about five: her white-blond hair is cut into a bowl shape; her bangs are cut a bit crooked. She told me that when the picture was taken, she was near the fence beside the barn. I looked around for remnants of the fence, but there were none.

The author's mother, around the age of five, at the old Murray farm.

As Bruce and I examined the area, the woman came back to the door and told us her daughter-in-law said it was fine if we wanted to stay and look around. A different dog ran out past her, barking madly at us. It was a friendly, excited kind of bark that caused no reason for alarm, and Bruce and I are both dog people. We thanked her, and, leaving the car where it was in the driveway, we walked toward where I knew my family's farmhouse once stood. The dog followed us.

Although the landscape looked completely different now that it was inhabited with new families, homes, garages, and landscaping—where there were once just open fields—I still remembered being there at age nine. I remembered us standing beside the remnants of a foundation and Grammie saying, "This was where our family farmhouse once stood."

But as we neared that spot, I could see that the area was now as overgrown as the back woods. Where there had once been only a few mature trees growing in and around the old foundation, young poplar and spruce now filled every available space. There was no path to follow, and I could no longer see any sign of that old foundation. We walked around, but although I knew we were close, I couldn't find it. It was hiding.

Disappointed, we crossed the field and walked toward the opposite wooded area and what I thought might have been Mona's Lane. Unfortunately, what looked like an old road on the aerial photographs was actually a long, narrow swamp. It wasn't Mona's Lane, but more likely the pond where my mother and her sisters learned to skate. As we walked along the wet edge, I felt even more discouraged that we had come to yet another dead end.

The blackflies attacked as soon as we entered the shadow of the woods. Although the bug spray did its job and they didn't bite, I definitely swallowed a few.

The dog was still with us but kept running off ahead, and I worried she'd get lost. "Dog," I yelled. She didn't respond. When I finally caught her, I checked her name tag. Aurora. She didn't respond to that name either, but I reminded myself these were her woods. She knew where she was going.

"We want to find land that's higher ground," Bruce said, as we moved farther into the woods. "They would have built on a high point of land."

This made sense to me. Although I knew nothing of building a home, it seemed like something people would look for, especially centuries ago, when scouting locations.

We walked around for a good hour. The only greenery on the trees were the spruce and pine branches and the new buds. No leaves were out yet. The ground was uneven, and sometimes I'd see something that looked like a path and we'd follow it. None of them led anywhere. I carefully examined groves of large trees, wondering if they could be the trees the quintuplets were buried under. But as I had discovered during my research, the land had been logged numerous times over the years by various owners, so it was likely that none of the trees I was walking around had been there 140 years earlier. Everything on the surface was different. Still, I paused by one large old spruce that had three giant rocks at its base and wondered—could that be where they were buried?

I noted that it was technically mayflower season. The rare Nova Scotia flower blooms for only a few weeks each year, and the dates range from early April to the end of May, depending on the weather. I knew my grandmother used to pick mayflowers along the Murray Road when she was a young woman. That road, also now overgrown, was on the opposite side of the neighbour's property, but still, I looked for the flowers in the woods. I found none. I did find a few tiny blue eggshells scattered about. Baby birds were a sign that spring was near, even if we didn't feel it.

I was constantly worried about losing Aurora, who kept taking off on us, so we started to make our way back to the house. As we neared the home, a man came out calling for the dog. He introduced himself and said his son owned the property but was out of town that weekend. He was dressed much the same way Bruce and I were, in long pants, a jacket, and rubber boots.

"We were looking for the foundation of the old Murray house," I told him. "But we didn't have any luck."

He pointed to the grove of trees across the field where our Murray farmhouse once stood. "I think there's an old foundation in there."

I told him about the two other homes that once stood somewhere on or near this land—Adam and Maria's house, which would have been somewhere in the woods behind his son's home, and also my grandmother's little guest house.

"Oh, I think there might be another old foundation in behind the garage," he said, pointing to a far corner of the property.

I felt a glimmer of hope. Perhaps this was the remains of the little guest house. It was close to the location of our Murray family farmhouse foundation, hidden as it was.

"I'll show you," he said.

Bruce and I followed him across the backyard, past a small garden and the flagpole, the former barn site. When he saw me stop and examine a little wooden cross near the edge of the woods, he noted it was his grandkids' "pet cemetery."

Once behind the modern garage, I could see what he meant about a possible house foundation. There was a hole in the ground that was too deep to be anything but man-made. I could see the stones from the sides of an old basement. Its original rectangle shape was lost, as some of the sides had caved in, leaving a slope on all sides. Trees filled in other lost spaces.

I was sure it was the foundation of Annie's little guest house.

Bruce picked up a large piece of metal that was partially buried under some weeds. "This might have been part of an old washing machine," he said, examining the find. Until the present family moved there, no one had lived on the land except the Murrays. Did it once belong to my grandmother? Or her relatives on the farm? It was likely. We continued sifting through the overgrowth around the foundation and discovered another find: a small, old-fashioned round bottle. It was clearly an artifact from a different time. The bottle was full of moss and sticks and mud. It looked like a little terrarium. It was a strange keepsake, but a memento all the same, and I decided to take it with me. I've since dried it out and keep it on my office bookshelf.

After a bit more exploring, including a walk down another old road that the homeowner thought might lead to something (but turned out to be an old logging road), I thanked him for letting us explore the land, and Bruce and I left.

Although I didn't find the foundation of Adam and Maria's old home that day, or the grave, I felt my search was over, at least for then. I had done everything I could, and part of me was okay with not finding much. I never expected the mystery to be wrapped up with a bow. I always liked the unknown aspects of the story anyway; it was what appealed to me as a little girl, and even now. The location of the farmhouse, like the grave, will remain a mystery.

What I did find was the story of my grandmother and her family on that same Murray land—slim threads of my family's past. I had spent quality time with my two aunts and felt a stronger understanding of the importance of family ties. As author L. M. Montgomery wrote, "Nothing is ever really lost to us as long as we remember it." I had literally chronicled my own family story and it felt like an achievement.

When I tell people the story of the Murray quintuplets, their real interest shows when I get to the part about P. T. Barnum wanting to purchase the bodies for his show. Ears perk up. This is where a little story from Nova Scotia connects to the world.

I took my daughter, Molly, to see the 2017 movie *The Greatest Showman*, based on P. T. Barnum's life. On the drive home from the theatre, I casually mentioned that Barnum had wanted to buy the bodies of the Murray quintuplets for his show. She had heard me mention the quintuplets before, of course, but this detail caught her attention. "Really?" she said. "Wow!" I heard her on her phone later that night telling one of her friends about our distant family connection.

This "small world" meets "big world" idea exists beyond Barnum. From the Highland Clearances in the 1700s to nineteenth-century midwifery, from historical death practices to Victorian-era photography, from multiple births around the world to the world-famous Dionne quintuplets, it all connects, in some way, to that piece of land in Little Egypt, Nova Scotia, and that one rare birth in February 1880.

Shortly after my visit to the old farm property, I invited my aunts Doris and Ginger and my mother to join me for brunch one Saturday afternoon in the spring of 2019. I had a stack of pages written about my grandmother and the farm, and I wanted to fact-check a few things with them.

Armed with my printed notes, I met them at a restaurant just outside the town of Pictou. It's a popular summer spot, looking out over the ocean. I was the last to arrive, which was no surprise to anyone.

We didn't hug, (we're not big huggers), but we did exchange compliments: "Don't you look nice." "I love your dress." "Great earrings." "Look at your tan!" Like Annie Brown before us, we are not a family who dresses casually. None of us would ever leave our homes without makeup and something at least a bit dressy, especially for brunch at a nice restaurant. Years ago, my mother and aunts' outfits would certainly have included heels, as mine did, but age had forced them into flats.

We all ordered a seafood dish, the restaurant's specialty, and sipped glasses of ice-cold water. I took out my pages and began by showing them the aerial photo I had printed out of the Murray property. They confirmed my suspicion that the foundation we had found was Annie's little guest house.

"Yes, that's exactly where the house was," said Ginger, pointing. Then, her finger moved north. "The other Murray house was right in there."

"I looked there and didn't find anything," I told them.

Doris shook her head, "No, it was farther back." She alluded to a piece of land that was much farther in the woods than we had walked. "It was in around here somewhere."

In hindsight, I probably should have showed them this map before my visit to the farm property. Or better yet, invited one or both of them to come with me.

"What about Mona's Lane?" I asked. "Where do you think that was?"

Although they had never heard the driveway to the property referred to as that, my aunts and mother studied the page carefully before Ginger pointed to the driveway into Bruce's brother's property. "It's hard to tell, because it's all changed so much, but it might have been in here."

Doris and Mom nodded. "Yes, around there somewhere."

I decided I might need to make one last trip to the property someday. But not anytime soon.

While I clarified a few points of my story with them, we mostly talked about our present lives. Fact-checking was really just an excuse to invite them to lunch as a thank-you for all their help. I hoped in the future we would do things like this more often, and that a lunch invitation wouldn't seem like such a rare thing.

As we walked out to our cars, the sky opened up in a torrential downpour. We exchanged hasty and quick goodbyes under wind-blown umbrellas. I hate driving in the rain and decided to wait in my car until the weather let up. As I sat there, I thought about the women in my family and what they had taught me: kindness, poise, independence, and the importance of family ties. These ladies may not bear the Murray name, but in my heart, I think of them as the Murray women, embodying the values that were passed down through the generations. For our family in Canada, it all began on that farmland. At least, that's as far back as the memories available to me extend.

Something about the day also made me think of my grandmother's mayflowers. Someone had recently pointed out to me that a mayflower has five petals—something I couldn't believe I hadn't realized already—and I had meant to tell my mother and aunts about this beautiful coincidence. Five petals, five babies. I had been searching for both all these years. I thought about actually looking for the flowers that weekend—the timing was right, it was still May—but I couldn't imagine where to start. Mayflowers thrive in wooded areas, where they can spread along the forest floor with partial or full shade—in Nova Scotia, that could be anywhere and everywhere. If any flower had the ability to hide, this one did.

It finds spots with just enough sun for survival but also ample shade to mask its location. Like so much of the story I had been chasing, they were determined to stay hidden. If I did find mayflowers somewhere in the woods—and perhaps I would someday, if I looked hard enough—I wouldn't pick them. Instead, I'd leave them to grow in peace, and tell no one.

When the sky eventually cleared, I decided to take the longer route to the highway, through the town of Pictou. As I passed the *Hector* replica along the main downtown street, I slowed and watched it rock in the dark, rough sea. I thought about the past for just a moment. I imagined the Murrays stepping off the old ship and onto this land for the first time, uncertain what the future would hold for them, and hopeful about the lives and the stories to come. Then I headed to the highway and drove home.

THE FOLLOWING DEATH NOTICE RAN IN THE *EASTERN CHRONICLE* IN FEBRUARY 1880.

(These typewritten pages were found in a relative's attic; they are based on an undated newspaper article. – LM)

Babies were perfect specimens according to newspaper account.

DEATH NOTICE

Murray – At Egypt, near New Glasgow, Feb.15, 1880, Elizabeth MacGregor, Margaret MacQueen, William Fraser, James Jackson, and on the 18th, Jeanette Rankin, three girls and two boys, children of Adam Murray. The five were born at one birth.

NEW GLASGOW, SEPT.9 – This death notice copied from files of the *Eastern Chronicle* of the time tells in brief the amazing story of Nova Scotia's own and only quintuplets. Years before it was ever realized that such a place as Callander, Ont. existed (outside its own community) N.S. was prominently and proudly pointed out as the home of the Murray quints. But the quints were born 50 years too soon to share in any small measure of fame which the Dionne quints enjoy. Now, from the musy (*sic*) time worn records the story of the Murray quints unfolds. Three of them lived an entire day, the fourth died on the following day, and the 5th lived until four days.

It was a cold blustery Sunday morning, Feb.15, 1880, the temp. near zero, when a messenger called at the home of Dr. Wm. Fraser of New Glasgow. The doctor was wanted at the home of Adam Murray, who resided in Egypt, a tiny settlement four miles away. They already had seven children and Mrs. Murray was again confined. Could the Dr. come right away?

Comments on the weather were exchanged as the Dr.'s horse was hitched and he prepared to attend a case of child birth at the Murray home.

To the tune of jingling sleigh bells the Dr. was off. After a brisk ride over the snow-covered lonely roads, Dr. Fraser arrived at the Murray's. There was the usual note of excitement in the home as the Dr. arrived.

Within an hour Mrs. Murray presented her husband with five children, all perfectly formed but very minature, the Eastern Chronicle report stated. Three of the children lived throughout the day and died that evening. The 4th passed away on Monday, the following day, but the 5th lived until the 18th.

"A large number of people have gone to see this wonderful progeny," the report said. But there was no indication that the birth of quintuplets had caused any stir of excitement far outside the small community. It was reported at the time, however, that a Yankee showman offered the parents a large sum of money for the bodies of the infants."

On Monday a small rosewood casket bore the tiny bodies of the four babies as they were interred. The fifth was buried the day following its death. The casket was one of many gifts from neighbors.

The mother, a strong healthy woman, a little more than 30 yrs. of age. had 17 brothers and sisters. Her mother, who was living at the time of the birth of the quints, had given birth to 18 children, including 3 sets of twins.

Persons who saw the quints described them as being positively beautiful. The dead babies were said to have resembled works of art in wax rather than natural born members of our race.

Took measurements

Official measurements were taken by the undertaker showing the size of the babies. The longest was 16 inches and weighed 3 lbs 4 oz. The second was 15¼ inches and weighed 3 lbs 6 oz. The third weighed 3 lbs and four oz. and was 14¼ inches in length. The fourth weighed 3 lbs and was 15 5/8 inches in length. For some reason the weight and length of the 5th baby was not given.

The father? Little was mentioned of him except the following:

"The father is an ordinary sample of physical development – in fact below average in stature and proportions."

A NOTE ON SOURCES

My purpose in writing this book was always to bring a little-known Nova Scotia story to life. I wanted to share the tale of the Murray quintuplets with the world. When I first started my research, I assumed I would simply be retelling historical events. I had no idea it would become a story about not only the quintuplets, but also about my family, my ancestors' land, and my own search for answers.

This wasn't an easy story to tell. My early attempts at research didn't offer up much. I encountered dead ends at almost every turn. Interviews with Murray family members brought no colourful family anecdotes, as everyone who knew anything had died long ago, and their stories had not been passed down through the generations. A trip to the Nova Scotia Archives proved mostly futile, as the main local newspaper from the week of the quintuplets' birth (the *Eastern Chronicle*'s weekly edition for Thursday, February 19, 1880) was missing in both digital and paper form. A search of the Dalhousie University Archives showed that although the negatives of photographer John R. P. Fraser seemed to be there, his famous pictures of the Murray quintuplets were not. The cemetery where they may or may not have been buried had lost all its records in a church fire. Nothing was panning out. It wasn't until I decided to look at what I did know, which was my own family's connection to the story, that I felt the book start to take shape.

There are many people who helped me pull this story together. Most importantly, my grandmother. Annie Margaret (Murray) (Brooks) Brown's interest in this old family tale is what started it all for me. I remember sitting in her living room when I was a little girl and being dazzled by the mystery of five wonderous babies, a circus showman who wanted to buy their bodies, and of secret, hidden graves. Although my grandmother passed away many years ago, her retellings of these events are still very much alive in my memory. She is at the heart of this book. There were countless times throughout my research that I wished I could pick up the phone and call her for an answer to one of my many questions. Instead, I turned to her daughters.

When I would ask my mother, Twila, and her sisters, Doris and Ginger, for information, they would start almost every conversation with, "I don't know what I can tell you," or "I don't know very much," when in fact they had a wealth of information for me. They simply didn't think it was important. But I was interested in hearing it all. I had no idea my grandmother moved to a guest house on the Murray farm because she and her new husband couldn't afford a house of their own, or that she stayed there alone with her young children long after his tragic death. It was during her fifteen years living on the property that she became interested in the story of the quintuplets. And my mother and aunts had stories of their own from the farm. These shared memories allowed me to piece together a picture of what life was like on the old Murray property.

Much of this book is based on memory. My memory, as well as that of my grandmother, mother, aunts, and others. Memory, as we know, can play tricks on us. For example, my memory of visiting the Murray farm as a child with my grandmother is vastly different than my brother's. In fact, he doesn't remember ever setting foot on the property. It isn't just faulty memories that create room for error, but also mistakes in historical recordings. One newspaper article I found said Maria Murray had seventeen surviving children, including three sets of twins, when in fact that was Maria's mother. Another said a sailor was looking to buy the bodies of the dead infants, when it was actually P. T. Barnum who made this offer. Around the world, newspapers ran stories about the miraculous birth of the Murray quintuplets and claimed all were doing well, but by the time the story ran, they had all died. Follow-ups were never printed. The same facts, based on a few original newspaper stories, have been printed again and again over the years. As there was never an interview with the family, information was likely from second- and third-hand sources, which allows for inaccuracies.

One of the fears I had about writing this book was that a Murray family member might feel it wasn't my story to tell. I am not a direct descendant of the family, and my connection could be considered too remote. There were people who wouldn't talk to me for their own reasons, and that's okay. I understand. The family stories I do have are as true as I could make them. I took every effort to confirm stories with various relatives, and recorded conversations for accuracy whenever possible. Dialogue from my childhood was written as best I could remember it. Any mistakes in this book are entirely mine. In most cases, the only way to prove or disprove facts would be to summon the sprits of my ancestors or to go back in time, neither of which is a viable option. I have tried to cover all angles and offer different scenarios as to what might have happened. Did the doctor arrive in time to deliver the quintuplets or was it my great-great-grandmother? Were the bodies really buried in the cellar of the home for a time, or was that just a story the family told to scare off grave robbers? And then, of course, the biggest mystery of all: where were they actually buried?

In addition to numerous pleasant afternoon interviews with relatives and extensive research (often with no payoff), this book is a result of my quest for answers. I always wanted to explore the woods of the Murray property once more and this project gave me the perfect excuse. I greatly appreciated the current property owners letting me look around, even though I just showed up at their door at nine o'clock on a Sunday morning. My hunt for answers also took me to local museums, including the Hector Heritage Quay in Pictou, the Carmichael-Stewart House Museum in New Glasgow, the Anna Swan Museum in Tatamagouche, and the Museum of Industry in Stellarton. Each of these museums offered not only important information for my book, but also allowed me to step back in time to better understand what life was like in Nova Scotia in the nineteenth and early twentieth centuries. I'm ashamed to admit that I had never visited some of these museums before, and I'm sure I'm not the only local person to say that. Yet people come from all over the world to explore our history. During my afternoon at the Hector Heritage Quay, for instance, at least three families of tourists came in wearing their own Scottish tartans for the tour. Display tartans are a big part of the museum. Before that visit, I had no idea what the Murray or McKay tartans even looked like. Sometimes we forget what's in our own backyards. Without these important institutions preserving local history, many stories from our past would be lost.

When it comes to tangible evidence confirming the Murray quintuplets' historic birth, there's very little. There is no mention of them in online lists of multiple births; they are not documented in scientific records and there is no headstone. There are, thankfully, old, yellowed newspaper articles about them. I found original stories in *The Eastern Chronicle* and *The Colonial Standard*, and other newspaper retellings of the same story throughout the years. Short stories about the quintuplets also appear in *Wreck of the Melmerby and other Pictou County Stories* by James Cameron (1963), *Notable Events in Pictou County* by Clyde F. Fraser (2015), *Pictou Parade* by Ronald H. Sherwood (1945), and *Along the Shore of Little Harbour* (1984). Other books offered much insight into some of the related topics I explored. For my chapter "Multiple Dimensions," I found Pierre Berton's *The Dionne Years: A Thirties Melodrama* (1977) to be particularly helpful, as well as British Pathé archival videos. For my "Memento Mori" chapter, much of my research was from Stanley Burns' *Sleeping Beauty: Memorial Photography in America* (1991) and Jay Ruby's *Secure the Shadow: Death and Photography in America* (1995). When it came to research for "Women, Midwives, and Witches," the revolutionary book *Witches, Midwives and Nurses: A History of Women Healers* (1972) by Barbara Ehrenreich and Deirdre English was particularly valuable, as was Dawn Raffel's *The Strange Case of Dr. Couney: How a Mysterious European Showman Saved Thousands of American Babies* (2018). My chapter "Everyone Loves a Curiosity" included research on P. T. Barnum from Dean Jobb's *Crime Wave* (1991) and Robert Wilson's *Barnum: An American Life* (2019).

Although the actual writing of this book was a three-year endeavour, I've been collecting pieces of research for most of my life. When I was young, and my interest in the story was first piqued, I remember telling my grandmother I would become a writer someday, so I could make this story famous. I'm not sure I've accomplished that, but I've told the story as well as I can. Hopefully I've done it justice.

ACKNOWLEDGEMENTS

Thank you to the talented team of professors and writers I worked with as part of the University of King's College Master of Fine Arts in Creative Nonfiction program. I graduated with this amazing degree in 2020, and without it, this book wouldn't exist. Special thanks to mentors Charlotte Gill, Ayelet Tsabari, Harry Thurston, Cooper Lee Bombardier, and Dean Jobb. Also, thank you to my first readers, Sue Nador and Joanie Veitch, and to my husband, Jeff, who was always encouraging and seemed to love even the early drafts. And finally, thank you to the amazing team of editors I worked with: Angela Mombourquette at Nimbus for her patience in putting together the final book, Stephanie Domet for her bigger vision of this story, and Marianne Ward for her helpful edits. This is ultimately a story about family, and I appreciate all the time my aunts and mother—and other Murray relatives—took to reach deep into their memories and help me retell this small historical moment in Nova Scotia's past. It is gratifying to know that this tale and the people in it will not be forgotten.